Apartments and Dormitories

Apartments
and
Dormitories

AN ARCHITECTURAL RECORD BOOK

McGRAW-HILL BOOK COMPANY, INC.

New York   Toronto   London

1962

APARTMENTS AND DORMITORIES

02202

8 9 10 11 12 13-NY-9 8 7 6

Foreword

THE skies are clearing for those concerned with the design, construction, and management of apartment buildings. During the past decade such activities were confronted with seemingly more than a just share of difficulties; partly social or legal, but for the most part financial.

In 1950 Thomas S. Holden—Vice Chairman of the Board, F. W. Dodge Corporation, and a distinguished authority on building economics—pointed out in an article in *Architectural Record* that the percentage of family consumption expenditures for basic shelter (rents or their equivalent, but not operating costs) had climbed only slightly above the low point of 9.28 it had reached in 1946. In a more recent article (included in this volume, pp. 2-4), however, he notes that this slight upturn gained such strength in the fifties that by the end of 1957 the figure for basic housing had reached 12.30 per cent.

Briefly, this means that more Americans now own, are building, or are renting more housing of larger area and of better materials and equipment than at any time for the past 20 years. Thus, for apartment projects, there exists a favorable economic climate which is expected to persist for some time to come. Building money—until recently tight—has now eased; a fact that adds a further encouraging note.

The apartments presented in this book have been carefully selected from among those published in *Architectural Record* during the past several years. They hold many ideas and suggestions which should prove valuable to the designers, builders, owners, and managers of rental housing.

Nearly one quarter of the book is devoted to dormitories and other college housing—a special type that is being constructed in growing number in all parts of the country. With the college population expanding rapidly, there is every reason to feel confident that the volume of such building will increase steadily and assume unprecedented proportions in the near future. Thus, the considerable material on college housing seemed appropriate and should likewise prove valuable to the architects, builders, and campus executives who will be carrying this large volume of work forward.

James S. Hornbeck, A. I. A.
Senior Editor, ARCHITECTURAL RECORD

Contents

.

I
Building Multiple Dwellings

ACCENT ON BETTER LIVING

By Thomas S. Holden, *Vice Chairman, F. W. Dodge Corporation*

Better housing has been a major feature in the spectacular advances in American living standards during the postwar period. While this has been a matter of common observation, it is also forcibly brought out by analysis of the statistical records of personal consumption expenditures compiled and published by the United States Department of Commerce.

Shelter Spending Increased

As a percentage of total consumption expenditures aggregate annual outlays for shelter by the nation's families have been rising continuously since 1946, as shown in Chart I.

It should be explained that the housing costs shown in Charts I and III do not represent the capital costs of new housing (which serves only a marginal fraction of the whole population), but they cover current expenditures for shelter as represented by rents paid by tenant families plus a calculated equivalent of rent (amortization, interest, taxes, etc.) for all the home-owning families. Housing costs, as here used, cover basic shelter costs only, not outlays for housing operation.

In 1946, first postwar year, only 9.28 per cent of the nation's total consumption dollars was spent for shelter. A long-time downward trend for this percentage had been in evidence since 1909, the earliest year for which overall data are available. (In 1909, American families had laid out for rent —plus rental equivalent of owned homes—a full 19 per cent of their total spending.) The downtrend was naturally accelerated during war years

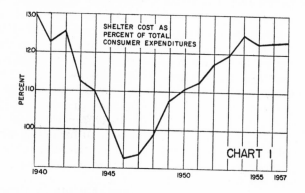

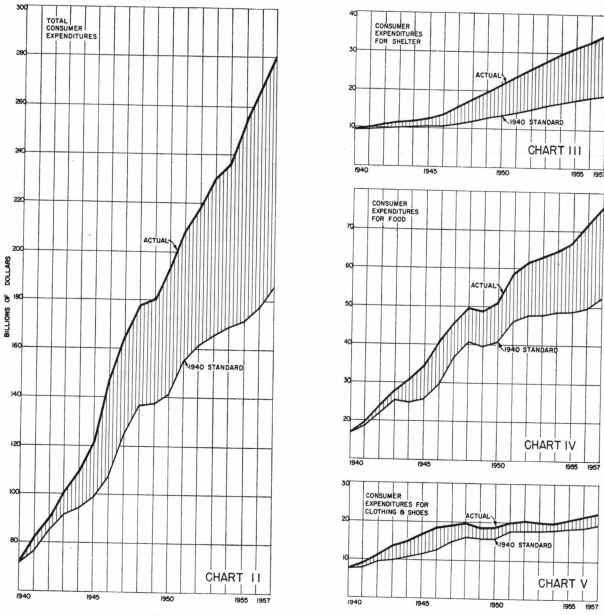

Data for charts derived from U. S. Department of Commerce figures

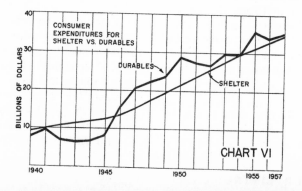

partly by rent control and partly by the fact that better housing was not available in a measure adequate to supply any considerable potential demand arising from improved national income. From 1946 to 1957 the percentage of total consumption expenditures allocated to housing rose from 9.28 to 12.30. This upward trend reflects a very considerable improvement for housing in the total consumption expenditures picture.

Housing Lagged In The 1940's

An earlier study by the present writer ("We Can Afford Better Housing," published in the September, 1950, issue of ARCHITECTURAL RECORD) brought out some interesting facts. It showed the first category of family consumption expenditures to rise as incomes improved after the great depression was food. A better rounded diet was apparently the most generally immediate desire when the opportunity arose for resumption of pre-depression living standards. Improved diet standards continued a dominant factor in the rising standard of living throughout the period of the present study.

The earlier study also showed that during the war years and for several years following, family expenditures for clothing and shoes exceeded housing expenditures; there were even some years in the late 1940's when combined expenditures for liquor, tobacco, and amusements exceeded expenditures for shelter. The earlier study indicated that the time was ripe for large-scale building of quality housing and a general upgrading of housing standards so that this category of facilities would catch up with other facilities, goods, and services being enjoyed by the American people.

Advancing Living Standards

The general advance in living standards, as shown in the records of total consumer expenditures, is pictured in Chart II. The year 1940 is arbitrarily chosen as the base year for comparisons; it serves as a prewar base, and it was about the time that the nation had regained the standards which had prevailed in 1929 and had lapsed in the intervening depression years. The lower curve, representing the assumed consumption requirements of each year at the 1940 standard, is made up as follows: For each year the actual 1940 consumption is multiplied by two factors, one to take care of the population increase of the particular year over 1940 and one to take care of the increase in the consumer price index over 1940. The excess of actual year-by-year expenditures over these calculated 1940-standard figures is indicated by the shaded area of the chart. The spread between the two curves is a rough measure of the overall improvement in consumption standards—the extent to which Americans were living better in 1957 than in 1940, and in the intervening years.

Housing Standards Have Caught Up

A similar analysis of housing expenditures compared with 1940 housing standards is shown in Chart III. In this the improvement factor (spread between the two curves) is small during the war years, but of steadily increasing magnitude from 1946 on. Charts IV and V show that there was a continued upgrading of standards in food consumption and in clothing and shoes purchased right through the year 1957.

In Chart VI is shown a year-by-year comparison between total housing expenditures and expenditures for durable goods (automobiles and parts, household furni-

ture and appliances, radio and television sets, boats, books, jewelry, etc.). For the first time durable goods purchases leaped ahead of housing expenditures in 1946, and have continued ahead through 1957. However, the spread between the two aggregates of expenditures has been very narrow during the past four years. As a factor in improved living standards, better housing has been catching up with durable goods ownership. Actually, during the 1946-1957 period household furnishings and equipment accounted for nearly 46 per cent of durable goods expenditures, exceeding outlays for automobiles and parts in all but two of the years.

Basic Factors in Housing Progress

Better housing standards in general have resulted principally from three factors:

1. The building of 12,903,600 new non-farm dwelling units from 1946 through 1957.

2. An upgrading of the home-building industry's product during a number of the years in question. For example, average floor area in new houses increased from 983 square feet in 1950 to 1230 square feet in 1956; the percentage of new houses with three or more bedrooms increased from 34 in 1950 to 78 in 1956.

3. The moving of millions of families each year into new houses and into existing dwellings of better grade than those they previously occupied. Recently, one person in five has moved each year, two thirds of them going to new addresses in the same county.

A Consumption Expenditure Pattern

The predominant importance in American family budgets of shelter, house furnishing and equipping, and household operation is strikingly illustrated in the appended table showing the nation's consumption expenditure pattern for the year 1956. (This is the latest year for which this detailed breakdown is available.)

1956 CONSUMPTION EXPENDITURES

(National Totals)

Housing (*rent plus equivalent*)	$32,841,000,000
Home furnishings and appliances	12,396,000,000
Household operation	23,717,000,000
Food	71,326,000,000
Clothing and shoes	21,813,000,000
Care of clothing and person	7,061,000,000
Automobiles and parts	14,572,000,000
Transportation supplies and services (*oil, gas, repairs, public transportation, etc.*)	15,742,000,000
Alcohol and tobacco	15,041,000,000
Amusement and recreation	13,844,000,000
Personal business	13,968,000,000
Medical care and death expense	12,793,000,000
Education, religion, charity, etc.	9,710,000,000
Durable personal effects (*jewelry, etc.*)	2,336,000,000
TOTAL	**$267,160,000,000**

It may be fairly concluded that the period here reviewed was one of extraordinary progress in raising the nation's housing standards. It also appears that the nation's pattern of consumption has achieved a better balance than it previously had in quite a long time, if ever. However, a population which continues to increase at a rapid rate and which has had its appetite for better living only partly satisfied will keep on demanding better housing as a vital factor in further advances in living standards.

HOUSING PATTERNS
AND WHAT MAKES THEM

Text and sketches by **Harry M. Weese**

The forces shaping cities today are complex and not as rational or understandable as in historic times. Housing forms the bulk of the city and is thus basic in determining its character, which in turn attests to the forces forming the environmental pattern. Were these forces and patterns satisfactory, our city dwelling would not be allowed to deteriorate in one or two generations. As it is, only a few patterns survive and acquire historic values to become monuments in the configuration of that accretion of human endeavor which is a lasting city. This is the story of the Old World. In its place we now offer a brave New World pattern of shelter based on our new society.

Originally we were an agricultural country of land-owners and strong families; our farmsteads grew to ag-glomerations of permanent buildings handed down through several generations, as were the dwellings sur-rounding village greens in the country towns. That was early 19th-century America. Industrialization brought en-larged cities which grew densely along tentacles of street-car lines and com-muter roads. The automobile further spread the city in the 20's and brought unprece-

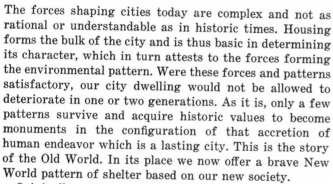

tentacles ..... filled in

dented disorder as well. Yet that sprawl was nothing com-pared with the expansion and migration caused by World War II. The new mobility of people and services spread the city far and wide and changed the emphasis from apart-ments to single-family houses, since the central city had used up its land and was hemmed in by surrounding towns.

Builders learned to deal in large quantities; project builders replaced the carpenter builders who, during the 30's, had erected—with FHA help—four of five houses a year on vacant lots in the arrested subdivisions of the 20's. FHA's timely legislation aided the orderly comple-tion of unfinished business, served to spur building activ-ity and home ownership, was suitable to the depression needs of the 30's.

After the war, in a climate of unprecedented demand, we went back to business as usual, with the free-standing house as the mainstay of new housing supply and the answer to the American dream.

While the cities stood still (except for some high-rent apartments and public housing), the fringe lands were quickly covered with houses built with government as-sistance designed for a different purpose in another era. The builders' lobby offered raw land development of single-family dwellings as the way* to add to the housing supply of the deteriorating and jammed cities. The gov-ernment would not insure mortgages for inlying city areas; instead, small-down-payment terms were offered to induce people to abandon them. This policy rejected the original premise that government would help when private enterprise could not. Rejected in financing im-provements of city dwellings and blandished by the monthly-payment-cheaper-than-rent, city folk in great numbers migrated to the suburbs. Development of fringe lands at the expense of central areas accelerated the de-terioration and abandonment of the city, accelerated the decline of mass transit systems, and aggravated highway confusion. Also, entire suburban communities became stratified in terms of family composition, age, and income, contributing to the dilemma of conformity. Yet, for those reared in the city there was no return to the city—for it continued to deteriorate.

Such is the process of income stratification under mass building techniques in large metropolitan areas. Contrast this picture with the smaller, older, integrated commu-nity or with the older pre-merchant-built community where land was subdivided to persons who built individ-ual houses over a span of time. Such communities are diverse and stable and can support wide variations in income levels. They are integrated, and their citizens put down roots. Growing up in such a town is a far richer experience than the stratified, nomadic, conformist way of mass-built suburbia.

Under present conditions we can achieve such diversity and integration only in the small, complete city or in the re-worked older communities of the central city, provided one accepts the basic proposition that we cannot build a city using one method, one philosophy, one housing type,

This does not take into account the brief episode of Section 608.

and one moment in time. Although techniques and costs have improved, the results hardly demonstrate the best way to house America or improve our cities. Urban life must be maintained, improved, and made attractive again. But this cannot happen if each generation knocks everything down and starts over. Nor can we run away from one mess to create another in a synthetic new town. We can build the metropolitan area only by fitting into a large, idealized concept the efforts of many—all devoted to preserving, reworking, renewing, and adding for each generation the best it can offer toward a living continuity on the chosen ground. This requires a philosophy, a plan, a discipline.

Let us consider some of the ways willy-nilly new construction increases the housing supply of metropolitan areas. Some of these—such as trailers and motels—are beyond the pale of what is ordinarily considered housing, yet have become domiciles for increasing numbers and are part of the total pattern we must consider.

Mobile Homes

Since mobile homes now command over one tenth of the new shelter market, we should examine their place in serving housing needs. It may be that trailers form a better housing pattern for certain income and occupational groups than the pseudo-permanency of the cheaper development. Life in a well-ordered trailer park appeals to certain people; it offers amenities many developments do not. Best of all, the park concentrates dwellings in half the space of a tract, can be tucked away under the trees and separated from the surroundings. Trailer parks should be hidden in the fringes of green belts or forest preserves. The mobile home should be made respectable, for it is an honest answer to the needs of transient workers, newlyweds, certain older persons, and those who simply do not like to settle down for long. There must be, however, density control and a way of planning for schooling and other community services.

mobile homes in ambush..

Motels

When motels include kitchenettes, they are definitely one-room homes. Located in many communities on the fringes, or even downtown, they are occupied on a semi-permanent basis and become housing units.

Free-Standing Houses

Converting farmland to four families per acre, thus hiking land values, is the prime incentive to raw land development. With government aid, this is now the predominant pattern. It is recognizable by wiggly streets going nowhere, close-spaced houses surmounted by a sea of roofs skewered with poles festooned with wires.

sea of roofs....

It varies from builder to builder—some split, some ranch, seldom two stories. The staccato repetition of closely spaced houses with false individuality seemingly containing standardized people is advertised by standard lamps in standard picture windows. The lack of focus in street pattern, of town center, of planned community facilities, of planned green belts or parks, and the over-all pattern which merges without break into the next, all evidence a mechanical approach to community building under mass-production methods. Landscaping is limited to a ruff of shrubbery around the house itself, while gardening is simply lawn mowing. These evidence the rootless conception.

The Row House

The row house offers a better use of fringe land for modest dwellings in the light of land saving and a more concentrated, permanent community. Regarded as un-American in the provincial interior, it has been the basic pattern in seaboard Boston, New Orleans, and San Francisco. The row house in these cities comes directly from early American tradition. Now, after much re-education, we are beginning to appreciate and use the row house idea again.

The row house offers economy, permanence, and a configuration which spells community. Row houses, as high rise, are thought of as belonging in a city. Standard zoning and financing keep them there, although with outward movement of industry there are good reasons for building them in the fringe. Certainly, row houses offer a way to save land for community uses and green belts, plus a way to build permanently at no premium. They expose less than half the façade of a free-standing house. Their other economies are well known, and tenant privacy is without question rediscovered in them.

One-Story Row Houses

One-story row houses are generally not the best solution, particularly when there is any site undulation, since the view is then largely roofs with vents, skylights, television antennas, wires, tar, and gravel. However, in some areas there is definite promise in the one-story row house of a type known as the atrium house. This age-old pattern has been frowned on by zoning framers, even in the very places for which it is ideal. An example is Fort Lauderdale, where regulations imported from the North forbid common walls above 6 ft and require useless ribbons of land between the huddled, slightly detached dwellings. Contrast this with Mediterranean or South American patterns in a similar climate. There, the street is a walled enclosure behind which fountains play and one can live in privacy within rooms overlooking the atrium gardens. The atrium house also has a place in northern cities for those who like the expansiveness of one floor and can afford the necessary 4000 ft of expensive land.

Two-Story Row Houses

If one believes the duplex (two houses masquerading as one) is a creature of dubious value, the first step toward urbanity from the detached house is the two-story row house—appropriate for densities of 10 to 20 families per acre. It does very well where it need not try to coexist with taller buildings, in which case it is improperly scaled in size and intensity. Such an environment (over 30 per acre) calls for the three-story town house. The early Southwest

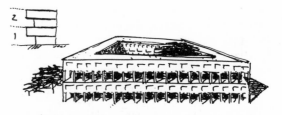

three story townhouses around a square

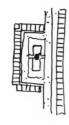

residential square SW washington

double maisonettes around a square

Washington residential square studies, seconded by the admirable Eastwick plans, show a row house pattern which uses land efficiently, provides separation of street, private gardens and commons, and creates commons that achieve an intimacy proper for groups. Row houses can restore the two-story house to grace. This pattern is proven by experience. Chelsea, Georgetown, and Beacon Hill are examples that demonstrate the lasting power of a housing type which has basic virtues and can be owned by its occupant.

On the negative side we have seen tenements built over stores on streetcar ribbons, court-type railroad flats at 90 per cent coverage, three-story walk-ups, and old-law tenements. These are incompatible with good urban living—past or present—and must be entirely rebuilt.

an outdoor room...

a square of three story houses...

Speaking of patterns, a further curiosity is the refusal of lenders, insurers, and zoners to countenance apartments and row houses in suburbia. Newly marrieds, old folks, and medium-income groups must leave town. Stratified thinking places likes with likes, while in reality, the country or fringe location is excellent for row houses. Scandinavia abounds in attractive examples.

Double Maisonettes

After two- and three-story row houses, appropriate for a density of 10 to 20 families per acre, comes the two-tiered row house (or double maisonette) at 40 per acre, 30 per cent coverage. There is no American word for this type, which has not caught on here because of the complex prejudice structure. PHA has forbidden it, private developers have never heard of it, and FHA is afraid of it, although it accounts for the majority of the London County Council's redevelopment effort. There, it is used both on the ground and in multi-storied tiers in their admirable postwar developments. A two-tiered row house gives you four stories for a three-story walk, plus through

views and ventilation, and everyman's castle has its own front door. It can be occupant-owned, either on a two-family basis or as a co-op. It is an excellent replacement for the obsolete three-story walk-up.

High Rise

When density exceeds 40 families per acre the sky's the limit. There are some large-city areas entirely developed in high rise to 300 families and more per acre. As Street-

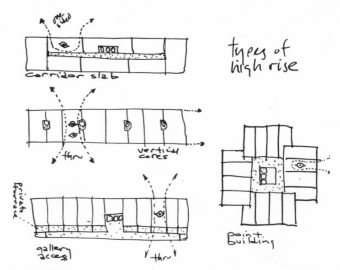

types of high rise

corridor slab

vertical cores

thru

private

gallery access

thru

pointing building

erville on Chicago's Lake Front demonstrates, when the once vacant lots used as interim open space, playgrounds, private parks, tennis clubs, and parking lots are built over, occupancy changes from families with growing children to doubled-up working girls, bachelors, and childless families. A degree of wholesomeness goes out of the area; it starts downgrade.

Unless growing families can be held, there is less chance of the city retaining those income groups which have a choice. Those with children who want to live in the city look for three things: a spot of outdoors to call their own, a community, and an equity. They would like a school as well, but the district lines as now drawn generally downgrade public education.

In town-house areas, high-rise infiltration can be critical. The entrepreneur usually builds as high and covers

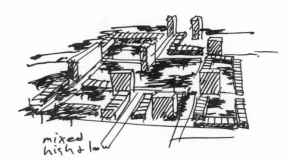

mixed high + low

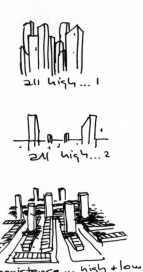

as much as codes and variances will allow. He probably means well, but the result is scarcely upgrading in terms of type of occupancy. The over-built site caters to a lower income occupancy, which drives older residents and owner-occupants away. When single-family occupancy in town houses falls below 10 or 15 per cent of population, the mixed pattern of high rise and town houses loses character and residential tone. The end result is either an arrested development of tall buildings mixed with rooming houses, or an over-dense area exclusively in tall buildings. Both patterns will lack children.

Local redevelopment agencies often tend to think of projects rather than communities and try to recoup write-down costs by maximum densities, creating redevelopment in the image of speculative venture or public housing. This, of course, precludes any of the graciousness of the streets of Bloomsbury or Bath, lined with trees and

the entrance doors of individuals. It precludes the attractive mixed high and low developments of the London County Council (Hackney and Picton-Camberwell among them), which reinforce the city core and acknowledge the desirability of urban living.

The loose texture of central London and Paris makes them habitable to the heart and brings these cities alive. It takes effort and leadership to secure proper coexistence of town houses and tall buildings which will bring that

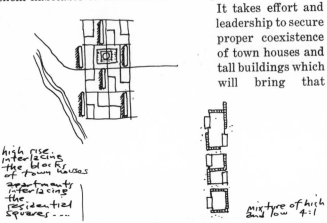

compromise between cliff dwelling and suburbia so necessary in attracting that element which is now deserting. But its achievement guarantees the city's future.

Another basic ingredient in the mixed pattern is walling-in streets to create street spaces. Sometimes,

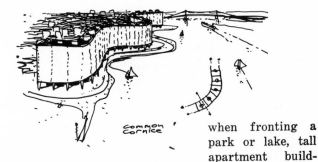

when fronting a park or lake, tall apartment buildings could come to a common cornice line rather than create an unoriented scatter in the image of free-standing suburbia.* Slab buildings with hotel corridors and single-exposure apartments are the style of developers. Exterior galleries and two apartments per elevator lobby offer relief from this pattern.

Public housing was conceived in a depression-born aura of concern for the slum dweller and midwifed by the social worker. We have as a result low-income ghettos of ever-increasing size permanently dedicated as such. This stratification is another example of the mechanical approach to housing and life itself that cries out for reconsideration.

The British can teach us a lesson: The London County Council redevelops London with more than the view of institutions for broken families and the lower elements of society. They regard slum clearance and city rebuilding as one, creating environments that can grow, appreciate, and become reinforced by social order. This is done not by establishing income maximums but by building for a cross section.

Who Makes Housing Patterns

Architects and clients have—in reality—very little to say about the basic shape and arrangement of buildings in which people live. The rules of the game hedge in the opportunities for creative innovation. Pattern is largely established by codes, ordinances, financing methods, federal regulations, PHA, FHA, URA, fire-insurance lobbies, health and safety lobbies, all operating on a national scale. This is demonstrated by the limited pattern developed here in contrast to the kaleidoscopic pattern of foreign cities working under different rules.

Since the only way to break out of the mediocre mold of our housing pattern is to break a rule, one can see how important it is that the validity of these rules is constantly under scrutiny. Modern architecture not many years back had to break down barriers of acceptance, and now housing architecture is facing new and subtle barriers. Housing design is hedged in, surrounded, and overwhelmed by a super-bureaucracy which would reduce everything to formula and put it on a punch card. We are trying to circumvent outmoded legislation framed by pressure groups. The effect has weakened cities while despoiling their fringes, as well as the small communities caught in the swelling tide of irresponsible development. The new laws must provide new incentives to favor the city, renewal and clearance funds to create sites, and an aggressive middle-income and cooperative financing program which can fundamentally influence the pattern. Otherwise, we will continue to fabricate a Brave New World no more interesting or livable than the punch card that fostered it.

*Consider Park Avenue then and now.

APARTMENT HOUSES

ONE HUNDRED YEARS OF SIGNIFICANT BUILDING

ONLY TWO APARTMENT HOUSES were nominated to the list of the fifty most significant buildings in the 100-year period (leading up to AIA's centennial celebration) which ARCHITECTURAL RECORD's panel of architects and scholars was asked to consider.

Both buildings were completed in this decade and both overlook magnificent waterscapes. Beyond this, and their basic programs, they have few points of similarity. The 100 Memorial Drive Apartments were designed by a team of architects whose principal stimuli were found, obviously, in the nature of people and the way in which they use buildings.

The Lake Shore Drive Apartments were designed by a single architect whose dominant source of stimuli has always been — and very evidently here — the generalized processes and materials of building itself.

Though widely different in intention, and in the situations provided, each of these buildings is a significant achievement.

Panel member John Burchard writes: "If posterity judges this aspect of modern aesthetics to have been an important one, it can hardly fail to assign preeminence to 860 Lake Shore Drive as the example par excellence of the attainment of a classic position. It is perfect in its proportions, serene in its stand. It states beyond contradiction that modern architecture has found functionalism not enough, for it denies functionalism both in the requirements it makes on living and in the admission as the new units will assert that to reveal a steel structure as being different from a concrete structure is not necessarily the highest aspiration of art. The questions 860 Lake Shore Drive asks are something like this: What more can be expected within this vocabulary? When will we learn to give such buildings their due by giving them a sufficiently complete setting, a question better worked out, if not better understood, in Rockefeller Center? How is a building so ordered to allow the individual tenant the freedoms he has a right to expect without the sacrifice of the overall dignity? This is of course a fundamental problem for society too but as yet at any rate our society will in such situations prefer individual chaos to communal order. Eight-sixty Lake Shore Drive reminds us again of this question. Its aesthetic brilliance transcends the expedient. It is a masterpiece then in more ways than one, and like a great piece of poetry has several levels of meaning."

Photographs on next two pages are Lake Shore Drive Apartments (Hedrich-Blessing), left, and 100 Memorial Drive Apartments (© Ezra Stoller), right

9

Hedrich-Blessing

Lake Shore Drive Apartments, Chicago, 1951, Mies van der Rohe. (Seventh)

"The Lake Shore Drive Apartments are significant as a successful esthetic spatial study of two multiple-story buildings on an American-sized square block. This includes the study of the ground level aspect and approaches to the site and the site itself. In addition this group is important as a concept of a thin outer wall construction (glass) on a steel frame embodying typical physical requirements. In some practical aspects the building has glaring faults, as many significant works of art do have. Within the limitations imposed by the law and other agencies necessary to its construction, these buildings represent an initial achievement of importance to architecture." **George Fred Keck**

"I must frankly admit that I am not an unbiased person when expressing myself about Mr. Mies. I have admired him when hardly anyone knew him or wanted to do so. The Lake Shore Drive Towers appeared like the wonderful conclusion of a lifelong aspiring formation of ideas. It is a moral force which sets the Miesian production apart; it is not mere formal abstraction. Young, and growing older, I knew and know more and more, it is the man behind the work who is the true impact to be esteemed." **Richard J. Neutra**

100 Memorial Drive Apartments, Cambridge, 1950, Kennedy, Koch, DeMars, Rapson & Brown. (Tied for twentieth)

"100 Memorial Drive sets a high standard of excellence from almost every point of view. It was designed for people to live in and appears to be delightfully habitable. The building takes full advantage of its site's major asset, view. With an ingenious plan, imaginative though simple handling of materials, mass, openings, etc., it becomes a well-integrated whole. It has also, I understand, been a successful venture for the client. This building is an asset to the community and a beautiful demonstration of good architecture. As is usually the case in a successful building, credit is due to the architects and to an enlightened and understanding client." **Hugh Stubbins**

Above is a view of a typical living room with its sweep of floor-to-ceiling windows in the Lake Shore Drive Apartments. Below are plans of typical apartments in Lake Shore Drive—two 3½-room apartments on the right and a 6-room apartment on the left

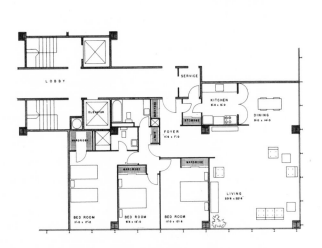

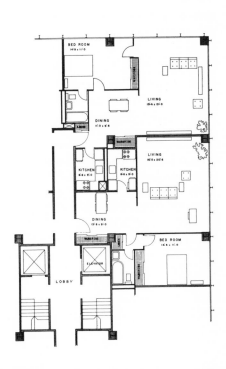

A PLEA FOR PERSPECTIVE

By Charles K. Agle *

WE ARE BLESSED with an incredible wealth of natural resources and ingenuity to get them out of the ground and put them to use. While much of this has had to be devoted to international conflict, there has been enough surplus to provide us with an abundance of material things, and our greatest domestic prosperity.

However, our living environment has not kept pace. Relative to the progress of other measurable wealth, it has actually receded. Our progress may have been so large and rapid that it has engulfed us, and we have not yet read its full significance or implications. We may be provided with opportunities that we have not yet appreciated and with tools that we have not yet learned how to use. In all humility, it may be wise for all of us soberly to re-examine our opportunities, the shortcomings of our immediate past, the forces at work, and see what to do with them.

THE FORCES AT WORK

An appreciation of the major factors influencing our physical environment includes at least these items: (1) continuing increase in population, and widespread need for small dwelling units; (2) the automobile as the major factor in circulation and land use design; (3) a powerful and prosperous economy, in which it is tragic to accept less than a decent standard of space and living quality; (4) four stages of family life, engendered by our mobility

---

* Chairman, Development Committee, National Association of Housing and Redevelopment Officials; Member, A.I.A. Urban Design Committee

and economic freedom, which require separate types of housing.

1. *Population change, both in numbers and composition, requires corresponding change in shelter and circulation.*

Our population has doubled in 50 years, and is still going strong (75,000,000 in 1900; 150,000,000 plus in 1950). Medical progress in conquering infectious diseases has lengthened life expectancy from 42 to 68 years — more than one-third — which means that more middle-aged and older couples survive beyond the marriage of their children, and return to a "two person family" status, with special housing needs.

2. *The automobile is here to stay.*

The number of automobiles has almost doubled in ten years (30,000,000 in 1943; 53,000,000 in 1953; and possibly 80,000,000 by 1975). It is no longer a vehicle of pleasure and luxury; it is a beast of burden for daily necessities of survival, and the sole significant means of transportation outside the centers of our largest cities. The environment for the automobile is now a large component part of the environment for the whole family. We must design for the automobile's smooth and efficient flow; for its storage; but even more importantly, against its hazard.

3. *Our building is permanent. Our physical standard should be based on needs, not merely immediate cost.*

The out-of-pocket cost of World War II, which did not hurt us economically, in spite of the fact that it produced no tangible asset, was about $300 billion. Its total cost, by the time we finish financing it and taking care of the veterans, has been estimated at over $1 trillion. There are about 50 million dwellings in this

Cartoons by Michael Ramus

country. In terms of real property, this means that, had we devoted an effort to housing equivalent to the effort we expended on the war, which we tossed off so briefly and ably, every family could have had a new $20,000 house, including a one-third down payment.

It seems to me that we have indeed lost our perspective when we absorb astronomical figures for armament without question, and at the same time reduce the space of our shelter, which is a trivial cost consideration by comparison.

It does appear that *there is no compelling economic reason for not getting what we want. If* we can make up our minds what we want.

4. *There is no average family. There are four major groups with different needs.*

It has already been noted that the group of people in search of a place to live is not necessarily the average natural family of five and a half people (two parents and three and a half children), but rather a median group of 3.1 persons. But beware of averages and medians.

The economic and geographic freedom noted above has given more practical significance to the fact that the "family" is not at all a constant, but a group of people whose composition and architectural needs change drastically at different stages. A study of census and other data indicates that there are at least four stages: (a) the formative period beginning with marriage plus about six years, when the couple are deciding where to live, how many children to have, and what they hope their income will be; (b) the production period of perhaps twenty years, when the children are all home and growing up; (c) a dissolving period when the children

marry and leave home; and (d) a static period of around fifteen years when the couple has the means to live well, but lacks the energy and the need for the old mansion. This last stage, of trivial importance only a few decades ago, now constitutes the largest area of need for which no specific solution has yet emerged.

THE SHORTCOMINGS OF OUR PAST

Much of our pre-war heritage no longer fits our changed circumstances. Even much of what we have done in the past ten years may return to plague us, though it can be excused because of the pressure of post-war population and its need for shelter. It is true that we probably have provided somewhat better shelter for *more* people than was done between 1900 and 1930, but the question still remains, is it as good as we can and should do?

What have been our shortcomings and difficulties?

Room sizes and unit planning

Our room size standards, as promulgated by both the FHA and the PHA in both houses and apartments, are such that it is impossible to walk on both sides of the

"The family is not a constant . . . but a group . . . whose . . . needs change drastically at different stages"

bed to make it. There is rarely any interior space left over for members of the family to get away from each other: in our middle and less expensive contemporary products, the house has virtually been fitted around the family like a corset — here is a tiny room (70 sq ft) you *must* sleep in, a nook to eat in (maybe) and a 150 sq ft living room where everyone must get together. Rooms are almost the same size throughout the unit and ceiling heights are uniform. In the mass of units, there is little attempt or success in really relating outside space to inside space through fenestration, grade levels, or design and landscaping of a private yard. The end product is a tight and monotonous series of little artificial cells in which there is no escape from social congestion and boredom, short of television or the corner beer parlor with juke box.

Site planning and common space

Most site plans, room placements, and side yards are such that we all live practically in our neighbor's laps. Cities have not kept up in providing parks and playgrounds and other open spaces to compensate for the absence of usable open space for the children on small lots. Any charm that streets once had is blotted out by double lines of parked cars without so much as a bush to hide their collective naked ugliness.

Failure to design a distinction between minor and arterial streets makes survival a sporting proposition with low odds.

Because of the black magic of finance and questions of title, it is ironic that the private housing program seems less conscious of the need for social space than the public housing program. In reducing room sizes and number down to the barest animal essentials, both programs have long since wrung out of the "unit" every inch of usable social space. In the public programs, at least an attempt has been made to provide *some* space in community halls, day nurseries, and kindergartens, and something in the way of playgrounds. In private developments, whether of single, or row houses, or apartments, this is seldom the case, because of the difficulty of communal ownership.

Misuse of building types

We have a tendency to miss the point of relating

building types to the various family programs. In the center of our cities, we force all families into high rise buildings because of land cost, but in the suburbs or in small towns we are usually forced by archaic zoning to scatter them all in cracker boxes. A clearer appreciation of family programs, and an understanding of the merits and demerits of various building types might help us steer around fallacies and confusion.

1. *The High Rise:* Both the children and their parents are underprivileged when the children do not have direct and immediate access to the ground, and playgrounds of adequate size and basic equipment and some sheltered play space within attractive range — not on the other side of town or down the elevator shaft. Without these facilities, the pressure and tension inside the dwelling is apt to run high if the children are healthy. The provision of these facilities in a high rise structure is just plain impossible. Density and land cost be damned: a child in an apartment is underprivileged, whether on Park Avenue, Lake Shore Drive, or the lower east side. The high rise building does have its merits, but not for active children.

2. *Row Houses, Garden Apartments, and Walk-ups:* We should first define our terms. A row house is an individually owned unit between plane party walls on a separate lot; a garden apartment is a collection of units in common ownership, in which each unit has a private outside door; a walk-up apartment is a group in which two or more units are entered from a common hall and outside door.

Most row-house developments, of which Philadelphia and Baltimore contain perhaps the dreariest examples, are characterized by rigid street patterns, complete waste of front yard space, which is too small for insulation from traffic noise or any private or individual use or landscape treatment, but which, nevertheless, consume enough of the lot area to rob the rear yard of any potential value. Rear yards either serve as junk heaps or are paved for parking off an alley. We thus have traffic and noise, fore and aft, no usable open space, no privacy, no view, and only the joy of ownership: but of what? While it may be acceptable for a sound-sleeping couple, what about children? Where do they play? Where can they even walk in safety?

The garden apartment has some better features than the row house, but generally fails to provide private open space related to each unit. Common ownership does make it possible for parking and garages to be grouped, and achieve some quiet near the living unit. Children at least can walk in the common open space, and some left over space may be available for playgrounds. However, the cost of retiring the owner's mortgage is a heavy price for the tenant to pay for the privilege of parking his car away from his unit and looking at a bit of landscape he can neither dig in nor sit on.

3. *Single-Family House:* Most fringe or suburban communities still hang on to the romantic fallacy that only a single-family house is good, and force all families into it, regardless of basic need. Proceeding from this vicious premise, it then becomes necessary to prostitute

lot and structure sizes in an attempt to serve families which, because of small size or economy, could be better served by other means.

"The end product is . . . a series of little artificial cells in which there is no escape . . ."

There is not much that can be said in praise of such developments of the minimum two-bedroom single house on a narrow lot, other than that it is a cheap and temporary expedient. Temporary, for two reasons: first, when hemmed in by narrow side yards and standard front and rear yard set-backs occasioned by obsolete zoning practice or lack of imagination on the part of the developer, its appearance can be as deadly as the usual PHA or 608 "Project," and it enjoys the privacy of a goldfish bowl. In standard examples there is little more private use of the open land than in row houses, and it fails to exploit its inherent advantages. Secondly, if we do not give the owner enough land to put up a carport and add a couple more rooms when children start arriving, he will soon have to abandon it. Although he may have had no choice, and was forced to buy in a seller's market, he isn't dumb, and won't spend a nickel on upkeep while he is waiting for something better.

It is therefore my fear that the too-small house on the too-small lot creates an inherently unstable neighborhood from the point of view of cold cash, disregarding quality, and that much of what has been built in the hysterical boom of the past 10 years is potential slum.

City Planning

There have been still other difficulties: the city plan (or lack of one) and the fast-buck subdivision. The first has inherited largely obsolete codes, ordinances, regulations, and concepts. When compounded with the best old-fashioned engineering and real estate thinking, this concoction has nicely supplemented the past neglect and indifference, or helplessness, of the architect, to give us our urban heritage: gridiron streets of uniform dimensions for all purposes in all directions and conceived

only for horses; sugar-lump houses of uniform size, height, set-back, and side yards so narrow that even a cat has trouble negotiating them, all nicely strung together in a tight row, with no outlook — past, present, or future; central business areas that are strangling because the automobile can neither get to them, or park once it gets there, all overlaid with flashing neon signs that give it the calm dignity and charm of a juke box.

Economic fears

Restlessness and insecurity may be aggravated by the mediocre quality of our three-dimensional life. This means more than the design of the house or apartment: we find that the city is no place to raise children because of the lack of play space, the over-burdened schools, congestion, traffic hazards; so we pull up shallow roots and fly to "the country." Then we find that commuting takes so much time and personal wear and tear that one parent is of dubious value to the family. Maybe it works, or maybe we can't find a suitable house in a good neighborhood within our means, and we move on to the southwest, or west coast, and try again. This rolling around may be aggravated because we can't find anything (collectively, house, neighborhood, schools, shopping, transportation to work, "atmosphere") that is good enough for us to want to hang onto.

WHAT TO DO?

What is quality in living? If occasionally we have stumbled in our quest, what improvement can we make? What opportunities have we missed?

The designers of living environment cannot stop with four walls. A few hundred years ago, when the major and compelling reason was shelter, the igloo plan of the Cape Cod cottage was an excellent solution to the immediate problem, and even the urban huddle was understandable. Today, however, we have the tools to do better.

What do we need? *Response to family personal and social programs.* This involves more than a listing of spaces of various minimal sizes: a psychiatrist's insight, an understanding of social habits, sleeping space for children, and space for them to lead their private lives.

It boils down to the major consideration of space. When there are a lot of human beings cooped up in one place, they get to be like the molecules of oil in the head

"Failure to design a distinction between minor and arterial streets makes survival a sporting proposition . . ."

of a high compression diesel. The internal pressure is in indirect ratio to the space, and when the space gets too tight the heat and pressure make them explode. If the piston is stuck and the exhaust valves don't open, the head blows off. This is my basic sociologic case for the one-story house on a quarter acre of ground for a full family, with at least one spare room to absorb the pressure on rainy days or winter nights, whether you call it a study, library, hobby shop, or just sparking space, to double for the youngster's jalopy when the roads are icy — and for the small family, at least a pleasant outlook to mitigate the tightness of a still smaller enclosure.

It is also highly desirable, in composing a neighborhood, to provide a balance of facilities for various family sizes. Only in this way can continued residence and the preservation of social ties be preserved as a family progresses from one stage to another. It also provides the best opportunity for architectural variety and interest through the use of proper building types for each family group.

Use of proper building types

The *high rise*, of course, has certain advantages which the low structure never can get — whether in a row or on an acre lot: fine light, magnificent views, and a feeling of great space. This suggests that it is really a superior building type for small families, whether it is located in the middle of a large city or on the outskirts of a village. Generally speaking, young married couples, either with no children, or children under, say, two, do not need the same access to the outdoors as larger families, and can do well without the worry of individual heat and utilities and the burden of landscape and structure maintenance. Except for differences in economic level and the ability to afford luxurious equipment, the needs of older couples line up quite well with the very young, and there is a legitimate use for high rise for these two groups. I only want to beg a balcony for everyone so that there can be some direct escape from the constant pressure of completely enclosed space.

Where land is not at a premium, a good case can be made for the garden apartment for these same two groups, the young and the old. For both groups, rental tenure has certain advantages over ownership, because no long financial commitment is involved, there is no responsibility or burden in upkeep, and its flexibility offers a good springboard into more permanent quarters for the young, and freedom for travel for the old. When nicely landscaped and built at low density, that type of short, but good, view is a worthy substitute for the distant view of the high rise.

Where the feeling of personal security is enhanced by ownership, or where private landscaping and sitting out terraces are wanted, a legitimate case can also be made for the often deplored *row house* — properly designed.

This "row house" needs brief explanation. Let us start backwards from the free-standing house and lot. I feel that walls with facing windows should be at least 20 ft apart, or the windows are worse than nothing

and should be somewhere else. This means minimum 10 ft side yards. The average small house that is habitable now has a breadth of about 35 ft, and we have to do something about attaching a car, for another 10 ft. Ergo, any lot narrower than 65 ft is small for a free-standing house, and it appears that about six dwellings to the net acre is tops for the houses that people want to build now. The hiatus between this six and the 15 where we can build an acceptable garden apartment is untenable. The first step in increasing density without losing any of the quality of the free-standing plan is to twin the garages with a party wall and save 10 ft. The next is to put a party wall on the other side and have all the windows front and back, still with the same one-story plan, for a width of 45 ft, but with still no serious loss in quality. With the sacrifice of one-story quality, and going to two, we still can have our car in the structure and have private and usable open space in the rear on a width of 25 ft, or a top net density of about 16. Beyond that the loss in quality is so abrupt that other building types — the garden or multi-story apartment should be used. Thus, with access, parking, and service on one side only, private usable open space related to interior planning on the other, and the superior privacy of a party wall over a narrow side yard, I feel that the row house can be quite acceptable on lots up to 50 or 60 ft wide, but that on lots narrower than 25 ft we ought to forget about it.

In my Utopia, this leaves the field of the three or more bedroom dwelling exclusively to the *free-standing house*, whether the floors are of teak or bare concrete. Quantitatively, this would be appropriate for half of the term of the average family cycle, and should be about half the total supply.

Site selection and full use of site planning opportunities

The architect, regardless of building type chosen, is constrained to design the immediate open space surrounding the shelter as part of it, and to relate his room sizes, shapes, fenestration, *and* circulation to the larger environment. It is not enough to provide the minimum of light and air essential to physical survival, as apologetically specified in building codes and zoning ordinances. We must have, as well, the variety and interest of something natural to look at, space we can see and sense outside our caves, and room to move about in a

"Both the children and their parents are underprivileged when the children do not have direct and immediate access to the ground . . ."

natural environment. As mentioned before, this presents a case for the honest "picture" windows, as distinguished from the current showcase; freedom of access to the ground; and a balcony for at least one room in every high rise unit.

Even all this is futile if a poor site is chosen, or one in which that ogre, land value, is such that there is pressure to overcrowd people.

With decent transit planning and installation, I see no theoretic, practical *or* economic reason for using a bad site.

The best site for housing is not flat, even though it may be cheapest to develop. Our thinking is handicapped by our heritage of easy walking on the valley floor. The flat valley floor is for farming, industry and commerce. The opportunity for light, air and outlook lies in the hills or along the water courses. Where neither hills nor water is available, the use of different building types in the same development becomes even more important.

Once we have a good site we must settle for no less than the satisfaction of four objectives: 1. The interrelation of structures so that they do not cut off each other's light, view, and privacy. The close juxtaposition of high rise buildings of equal heights in cities ranks with four foot side yards in the suburbs as being twin inexcusable stupidities; 2. Proper control of scale: specifically, the avoidance of long sight lines along streets where too much can be seen at one time and the visible repetition of many similar structures produces monotony. It is important that we have curved streets to control sight lines and a progression of scales on the way home, and that the last should be a quiet loop or cul-de-sac; 3. A modern articulated street pattern, in which *arteries* have no parking, limited intersections, and give no access to abutting property; in which *collectors* have no parking, give no access to abutting property, and serve only to distribute traffic to the minors; and in which *minors* are short and give the sole access abutting property, and serve only for designation traffic; 4. One or more focal points giving identity to the neighborhood as well as functional convenience: the elementary school, shopping center, the church and social facilities.

The atmosphere of the city

It should not be necessary to labor the point of esthetics with the architects and planners who design our environment. Suffice it to say that composition, variety, interest, and even beauty, *are* possible in our cities, and the need for these is more practical and compelling than is evident from our neglect. In other commercial fields, it is the practical support for success: the buyer of a car is much more concerned with its appearance than he is with the ratio of the differential. From that hard-headed point of view, again, a "good address" is synonymous with stable property values and atmosphere.

Some useful tools are already at hand, and others can be found, only for the price of looking. Starting at the center, we *can* have a village green, nicely planted,

"The igloo plan of the Cape Cod cottage was an excellent solution to the immediate problem . . . ."

maybe with a fountain and flowers instead of a surplus World War I howitzer; shops with sheltered arcades such as have been standard in Europe for centuries; a pleasant outlook and surroundings for our office or factory; a conveniently located parking lot with screen planting; an arterial parkway without billboards and neon lights.

Thus we can have a variety of changing and pleasant experiences: the view from our office, the shaded arcade (maybe even a cup of coffee at a sidewalk cafe); the green with its flowers; the parkway along the brook; the easy collector where houses begin to appear between the trees, and the small scale peace of our own secluded street. Add to that a private living space where the sheltered and open spaces are both part of a single composition, there is some variety in the scale of rooms, there is a playground nearby, and we have space to live, indoors and out.

While this concept obviously should be accompanied by soft music, it is also possible that is the best approach to a sound long-term investment — regardless of whose money we use, or on what terms.

In all of the foregoing I have tried to outline some of the specific aspects of the quality of total environment, as distinguished from the usual fractional preoccupation with a building. I have also tried to point out some of our past inadequacies as a means of searching for improvement, and have tried to simplify a statement of our problems and opportunities. I have no illusions about the existence of practical obstacles, the cold clammy hand of stratified government and financial interest rates, or the confusion and inertia inherent in specialized interests, professional, as well as business and social.

However, this is America, and we are strong enough to shape our own destinies if we can achieve a common understanding and desire. Our living environment has not kept up with our material wealth. Architects and planners can explain what we *can* have. We can get what we want.

COST OF MULTI-STORY BUILDING CAN BE CUT

By Bruno Funaro, A.I.A., of Howard T. Fisher & Associates

THE steady increase in building costs is of greatest concern to the designers and builders of low-rent apartment houses. To offset these increased costs, room sizes have been decreased, comfort standards reduced.

There is no easy way to lower costs without lowering living standards still further. It is necessary first to appraise the real human needs, then consider how these may be most economically satisfied by integration of planning, structure and equipment, rather than by more "surgery."

Recent buildings (a few of which are shown on the opposite page) indicate some fresh and pregnant ideas for reducing the cost of apartment houses. To promote research in this direction beyond the scope possible for the individual the Housing and Home Finance Agency has called upon Illinois Institute of Technology and Howard T. Fisher & Associates to study all phases of the design of multi-story apartment houses in order to find ways in which construction and maintenance costs may be reduced and the quality of livability improved. *

The researchers have decided to concentrate their initial effort on a new evaluation of those planning techniques and building products which have not yet been generally accepted for use in multi-story apartment houses. Most favored, of course, will be those which require the least use of critical materials urgently needed for the defense program.

Under most careful study at present are concrete skeleton frame, steel skeleton frame, exterior bearing walls of concrete or reinforced masonry with or without interior columns, modified cellular construction primarily without beams or columns, and curtain wall construction. Prefabricated floor and wall units and simplified plumbing and heating units will be studied.

Present research is centered upon a typical T-shaped plan developed by the Chicago Housing Authority and also upon an alternate guinea-pig plan developed by the researchers (see pages 22-23). This plan is specifically intended for the study of those building techniques and materials which would not be equally suitable to the Chicago Housing Authority plan. It appears to the researchers at present that construction economies might be achieved with a thorough integration of plan and a simplified structure, the repetition of units and the use of standardized prefabricated elements.

*This article is based on a progress report on Housing and Home Finance Agency's Research Project No. 1–T–99 conducted under contract by Illinois Institute of Technology, Prof. E. I. Fiesenheiser, Project Director, Howard T. Fisher & Associates, Inc., Architects and Industrial Designers, Subcontractor. The substance of this research is dedicated to the public. The accuracy of all statements or interpretations is solely the responsibility of the author. Statements may be altered by further investigation.

ROOM AREA (SQ FT) IN:	1949	1951
Living Room	150	145
Kitchen and Dining	90	70
Bedroom	125	120

Room sizes go down

Minimum room sizes for one-bedroom apartments in P.H.A.-aided low-rent housing; however the 1951 room sizes are greater than those used in 1942

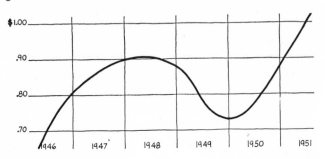

Costs go up

Average construction cost per cu ft: New York Housing Authority

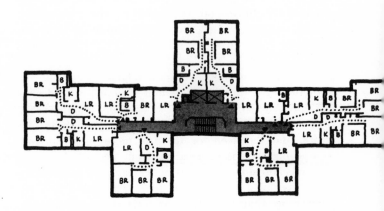

Ten apartments on a single elevator core inevitably produce long corridors and lack of cross-ventilation for some apartments, even when the building has been most skillfully designed. Lillian Wald Houses, New York Housing Authority. F. L. Ackerman, L. Goldstone, architects

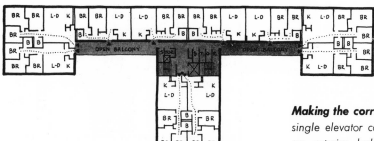

Making the corridor useful. Again ten apartments served by a single elevator core, but the connecting corridor becomes here an exterior balcony. This allows good cross-ventilation of all apartments, is also a place for parents to gossip and children to play on rainy days. Ogden Courts, Chicago Housing Authority. Skidmore, Owings & Merrill, architects

Skip-floor elevator systems, where a limited number of corridor floors, served by elevator, are connected by stairs with the apartments above and below, make it feasible to serve a large number of apartments from a single elevator core, without much waste corridor space. The corridor floors are clearly revealed by continuous horizontal windows across the facade. This building is by no means low-rent housing, but the skip-floor scheme with its combination of potential savings through reduced public corridor area and the added amenity of double exposure for all those apartments which are on the non-corridor floors suggests its applicability to low-rent apartment houses. Eastgate, Cambridge, Mass: Brown, Koch, Kennedy, De Mars and Rapson, architects

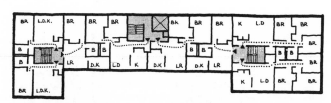

Typical floors (2, 3, 5, 6, 8, 9, 11)

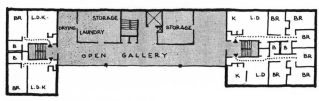

Elevator stop floors (4, 7, 10)

Corridor floors house community services in a low-rent apartment house with skip-floor elevators for the St. Louis Housing Authority. This adds amenity to cost saving. A 16-per-cent saving over a typical cross-shape plan is estimated: 12 per cent of this is due to less corridor space and the elimination of basements (the usual basement service areas are now on the corridor floors); the other 4 per cent is due to fewer elevators, simpler structure. Hellmuth, Yamasaki & Leinweber, architects

To evaluate possible cost savings in the planning, materials and equipment which go into a multi-story apartment house, the researchers sponsored by the Housing and Home Finance Agency (as described on the preceding pages) have evolved an alternate guinea-pig plan as a base for cost estimating.

This plan, as shown on this and the opposite page, derives from the typical three-story walk-up unit with one apartment on each side of the stair hall. This has the advantage of structural simplicity. It is well fitted for incorporating either a conventional frame structure, or some cellular system of interior bearing walls (see illustration at right), which allow the exterior walls of the building to function as merely a protective skin. Such a plan is also well suited to the use of standardized repetitive building elements. Each apartment here has cross-ventilation; there is a minimum of space wasted on corridors; and, unlike the plans of many recent housing projects, the living room here does not have to double as a connecting corridor within the apartment unit.

It has been found possible to transfer this plan, with all its advantages, to the high-rise apartment house. To avoid the unjustifiable expense of one elevator shaft serving only two apartments on each floor, it follows naturally that this plan should be combined with the skip-floor system of elevator layout.

In the proposed high-rise building shown here, community facilities such as laundries, drying yards and play areas would be provided on every fourth floor, where the tenants could reach them without having to go outdoors. The elevators would stop only on these floors and stairs would lead from this corridor floor to the apartments one flight up or two flights down.

In addition to the community facilities on these corridor floors there will also be space for a number of one-bedroom apartments. These increase the variety of accommodations within the building, and are particularly valuable for elderly people who cannot be expected to use the stairs. As a cost control, this plan is believed to be of extremely practical value.

In high-rise version, corridor floors house tenant services

The three-story walk-up plan, with all the previously mentioned inherent advantages, has been translated into a high-rise apartment house by piling up a number of three-story units vertically one above the other. Corridor floors are used as the filling in this sandwich.

All the necessary horizontal lines of communication are concentrated on the corridor floors, also the various community facilities which in a standard apartment house would be put in the basement. Each corridor floor becomes the play and service yard for the tenants of the three-story slice.

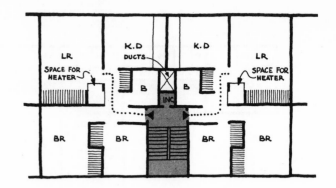

The unit plan

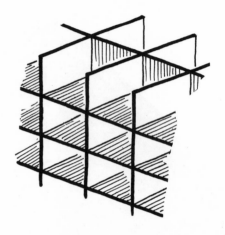

Modified cellular construction with bearing interior walls

Play area in a corridor floor

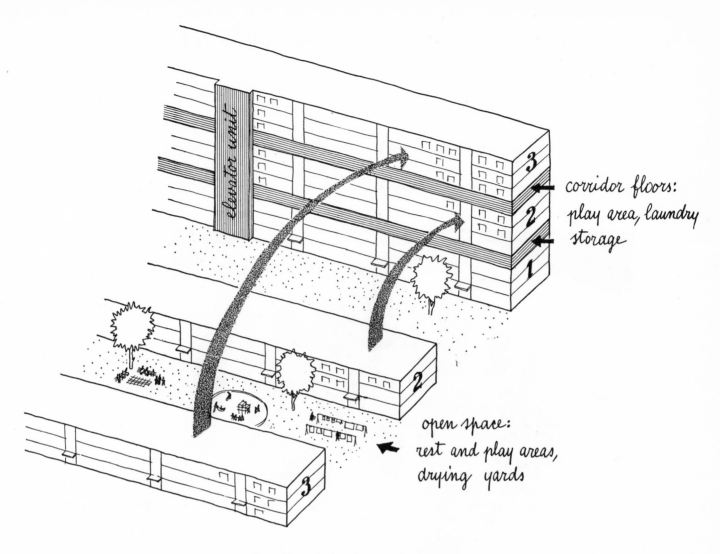

corridor floors: play area, laundry storage

open space: rest and play areas, drying yards

Diagrammatically shown above is the translation of the typical three-story plan to a high-rise apartment house with-community services on corridor floors. **Developed into a ten-story apartment house** (below) and fitted with skip-floor elevator system. Tenants may go one flight up or two down to reach a corridor floor

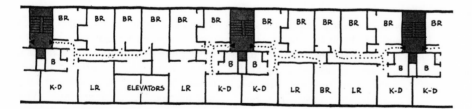

Non-corridor floor (2, 3, 4, 6, 7, 8, 10)

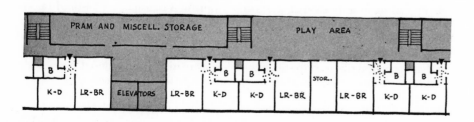

Corridor floor (5, 9)

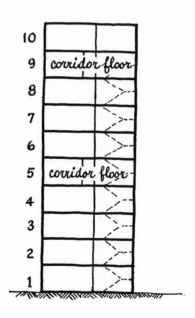

Section

PARTITIONS FUNCTION AS COLUMNS

In Scheme For Apartment Buildings

Olgyay and Olgyay, Architects, Notre Dame University

Bela Kiss, Structural Engineer, Budapest   *Comments by Paul Weidlinger*

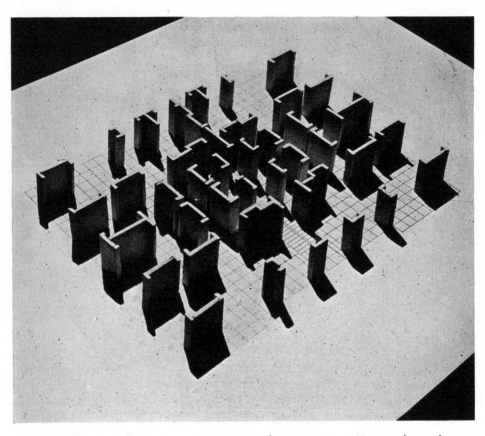

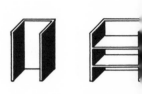

Various types of par...

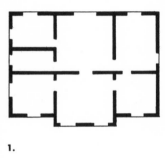

1.

Model of floor in walk-up-type apartment pictures how concrete partitions work as columns

THERE is a growing tendency in some phases of building, just as there has been in the aviation and automotive industries, to depart from "frame and enclosure" types of structures—that is, those structures which separate load-bearing elements from the rest of the construction. For example, "stressed skin" type of construction employed in airplanes also has found application in load-bearing plywood walls for prefabricated houses.

Architects, Olgyay, and engineer, Bela Kiss, have encouraged this tendency with their system of multi-story construction: *reinforced concrete partition walls become the supporting elements, eliminating separate columns.* Broken shaped partitions, especially suitable for apartments, and two-way ribbed floors work together to carry imposed loads.

Efficiency of building construction often is expressed on the basis of ratio of total dead load to utilizable live load — efficiency varying inversely with this ratio. The system of construction presented here, called *cellular* by the architects, is aimed at reducing this ratio to a practical minimum.

Partitions, by virtue of their shape, obtain maximum utilization of strength of materials, following somewhat the idea of light gage steel construction. The partitions are functional otherwise in that horizontal ribs used to stiffen the vertical sections can serve as shelves.

System Originated in Europe

This method of construction is one of the many advanced methods which have

come to us from Europe, where the importance of saving materials has given the impulse to a number of new developments. Innovations, based on an economic system and material and labor cost relationship which are quite different from ours, often are not suitable to adaptation here.

Of many such ideas, only those which represent fundamentally new and sound structural concepts are destined for application in the U. S. The recent successful "Americanization" of prestressed concrete is an example of this. *Cellular* construction, if introduced here, might become the next contender.

What's New About It

It is in many respects a basic development in the spirit of advanced building technology. These are as follows.

1. It is the next logical step in development of the flat slab, which represented the transition from linear column-girder construction into the three dimensional rigid frame.

With *cellular* construction, the linear, one-dimensional column is replaced by the two-dimensional wall. (It is interesting to note the reappearance of the "load-bearing" partition in its new form.)

2. In the quest for elimination of all unnecessary weight from structures, full utilization of new building materials of high strength and uniformity has become a problem. Structural elements are now reduced to critical cross-sectional areas; and instead of strength, elastic stability (i.e. the over-all or local buckling of the members) becomes the controlling factor in design. This is clearly expressed, at present, in structural elements and shapes developed for light gage steel, aluminum and also plywood.

The very same problem is faced and solved now in this new method of construction in reinforced concrete. Load-bearing elements are thin-walled concrete shapes, stiffened to avoid local buckling through stiffening flanges very similar to those of light gage steel studs (see top drawings on this page).

3. Structurally, this system is one which only a decade ago would have been nearly impossible to analyze. Even today, the design of a flat slab with irregularly placed supports requires a complex and time consuming analysis. The design of a slab supported and restrained by irregularly placed thin wall sections is even more complex.

Similarly, the design of concrete wall sections to avoid over-all torsional and local buckling is no simple task. However, the challenge presented by these problems can be met today with advanced methods of engineering analysis, but would not have been practicable a short time ago.

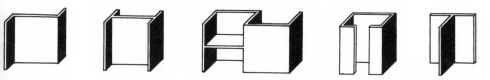

signed to get high strength and consequent thinness of section using reinforced concrete

4. Finally, because of the complexity of the engineering analysis, successful application of this system requires the disciplined approach and structural understanding of the contemporary architect. It is a structural system which requires honest architecture.

All these are sure signs that one is faced here with a fundamental innovation which is bound to have beneficial influence on our building technology, if it is given a chance for application in this country. The advantages to be gained are clearly shown in the two apartment house designs that follow: one, an elevator-type and the other, a walk-up type. These buildings were projected originally for the rebuilding program of Budapest, Hungary. The apartments actually built were modified because of the urgency for residential construction and the economic situation abroad.

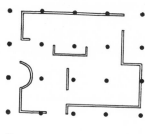

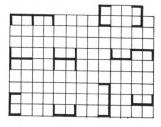

2.   **3.**

Comparison of conventional framing with cellular construction

1. The load-bearing wall system utilizes all faculties of the material: bearing capacity, space enclosure and insulation value. Between limits it is still the most economical. But above a certain height, it becomes impractical because of necessary wall thickness. At the same time, its cumbersome nature makes free planning quite difficult

2. Skeleton framing yields the essential advantages of economy in floor space, flexible planning and light structure. However, walls function only for space enclosure and insulation. Structurally they are only dead loads

3. Scheme of cellular construction. Vertical concrete slabs in various shapes act both as load-bearing elements and walls. They can be shaped, within a certain discipline to the grid, to fit a desired plan. Floors are two-way beams poured monolithically with the partitions. Structure thus works in all three dimensions. Forms may be permanent, providing both insulation and facing

How Apartments Are Built

Concrete partitions are poured in forms (or molds) which remain in the construction; molds serve as internal insulation and outside finish. Before concrete is poured, vertical and horizontal reinforcing is inserted in the molds. The molds are expanded gypsum and lime. Concrete in contact with the molds loses its water content and gets rigid immediately, shrinkage being less than in normal concrete construction. Molds are prefabricated in various shapes to permit precise and easy placement of the reinforcing.

Floors are grids of two-way beams with the open spaces being filled by hollow-core gypsum blocks. First these blocks are laid on formwork, and then concrete for the beams is poured in between. Where partitions are located, the beams are poured monolithically with them.

In a six-storied apartment in Budapest, the load-bearing partitions were built 2 to 3½ in. thick. Spans of the floor grid varied, with 24 ft as maximum.

Care has to be taken in design that the load-bearing partitions are placed in more or less equal "density." Due to the two-way floor grid it is not necessary that they line up. The amount of reinforcing necessary depends on how close partitions are spaced.

Implications for U. S.

Material saving aspects of *cellular* construction should gain added importance in the present economic situation. The feasibility of low cost walk-up apartment buildings in fire-resistant construction should be welcomed by all, including city planners and insurance companies. Elimination of all columns means increased floor area. Reduced depth of floor construction means reduced building height. Lightness of structure means smaller footings. All these spell more economical construction.

Many details of this system need modification and simplification to reduce the amount of hand labor required in its present form. The floor could be designed and built like our present "flat plate" construction or like the two-way concrete joist systems, such as the so-called "Grid System."

Wall sections possibly could be precast in standardized sections, or special steel forms might be developed. The European method of using permanent forms which serve as a finished wall surface could also be well adapted to our needs.

Simplified Design Method

Before general application can be attempted, a simplified method of design acceptable to building codes needs to be developed. This should not be 'too difficult, with present methods of experimental stress analysis. Recent commercial availability of the photo reflective stress analysis (*Presan*), developed especially for flat slab design, would seem to be adaptable to this type of work. As a matter of fact, it seems very likely that an adapted form of the *cellular* construction should bring about quite a few simplifications in both design and building in reinforced concrete.

ARCHITECTS' DESIGN FOR ELEVATOR-TYPE APARTMENTS

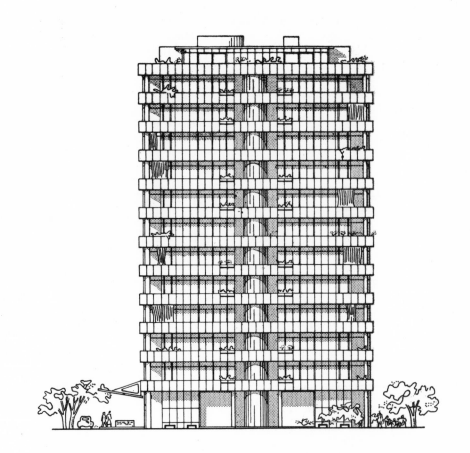

ARCHITECTS' DESIGN FOR WALK-UP-TYPE APARTMENTS

Elevator-type building designed with 12 floors. Four apartments on each floor are symmetrically arranged around the elevator lobby. The fire stairs are located outside the building itself, being accessible from terraces off the kitchens. There are four mechanical cores going through the building, ventilated by a central fan at the top

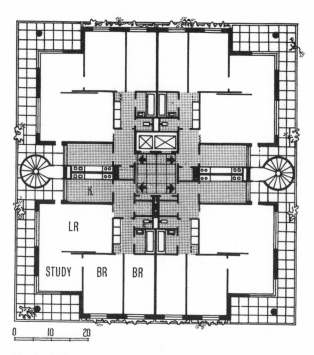

Typical Floor Plan

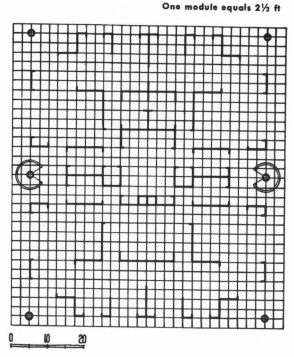

Plan of Load-bearing Partitions Only

Walk-up-type building with three floors. Each floor has two, 2-bedroom type, and two, 1-bedroom type apartments. Service areas are in the interior, and living areas around the edge; mechanical equipment is in two cores. Outside wall area is only 65 per cent of floor area

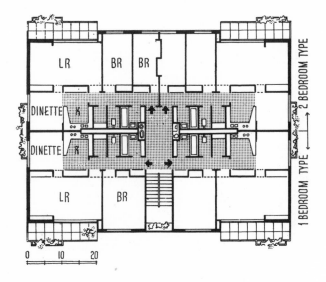

Typical Floor Plan

One module equals 2½ ft

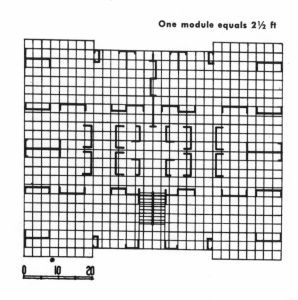

Plan of Load-bearing Partitions Only

ARCHITECTS' DESIGN FOR ELEVATOR-TYPE APARTMENTS

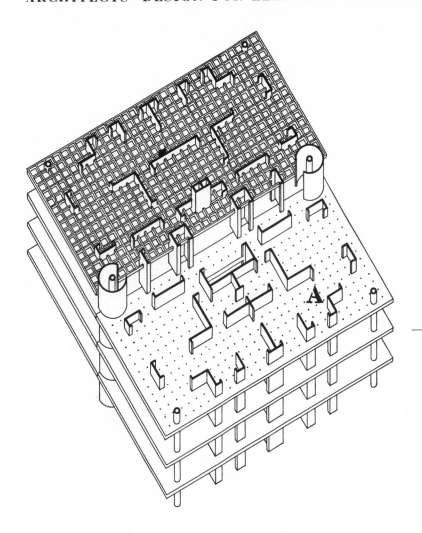

Upper floor in this structural sketch shows the two-way beam grid and how the load-bearing partitions lace through it. In the system as proposed for use in Europe, hollow core gypsum blocks fill in the spaces between the beams. These blocks may be left out to provide space for lighting fixtures. Ceilings are plastered and various types of flooring materials may be placed on top of the blocks. Partition "A" is shown enlarged at right

ARCHITECTS' DESIGN FOR WALK-UP-TYPE APARTMENTS

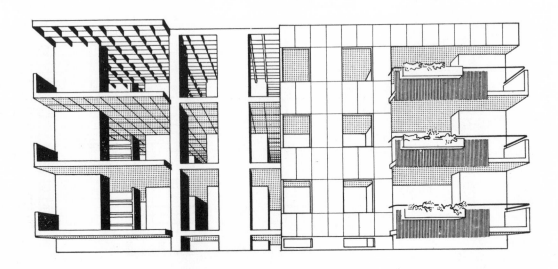

Perspective showing structural and facing elements of construction

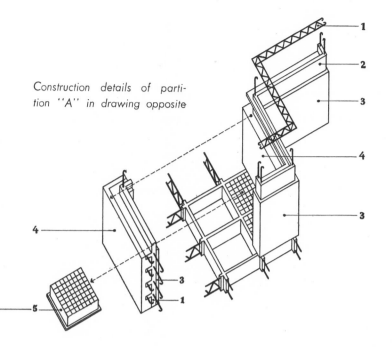

Construction details of partition "A" in drawing opposite

Top photo: apartment similar to ones illustrated on foregoing pages, but designed with fewer amenities for lower cost. Middle load-bearing walls are "U" shaped, with horizontal ribs being used as book shelves. Note glazed lighting strips which are easily formed in hollow spaces left in the ceiling. Bottom photo: here the load-bearing walls form cupboards. Spaces between them are filled with movable glass panes; glazed tile is underneath. Outside walls have one row of glass block at top

INDIVIDUAL APARTMENT HEATING
FOR MULTI-STORY HOUSING

By Robert K. Thulman, Housing and Home Finance Agency, and
Robert L. Davison, Howard T. Fisher & Associates

REGARDLESS of what form housing may take, be it a huge slum clearance apartment building, a Greenbelt town consisting of a mixture of individual houses, row houses, and apartments, or a rural development of small farm houses, the fundamental heating problem is always the same. It is to provide heating equipment at a first cost consistent with the cost of the project, which, with reasonable care and attention, will maintain proper and acceptable comfort. And the operating and maintenance cost should be within the range of what the occupants of the project can afford.

This appears to be a simple problem, but when the heating engineer asks how much money he can spend, complications arise. From that time on, arguments, debates, and differences of opinion multiply with astonishing speed. When the heating engineer points out that excessive and poorly located glass areas make efficient and comfortable heating impossible, and that cheaply made windows will cause troublesome drafts, his remarks frequently fall on deaf ears. But when he translates window sizes, wall construction and infiltration factors into dollars and cents, the debatable points begin to clear up.

How Heating Design Progressed

Conventional practice in the design of heating systems for multi-family and especially multi-story projects has undergone radical change in the past fif-

teen years. There have been sweeping changes in architectural design, and changes in heating have followed changes in architecture.

The heating system for the typical six-story apartment house of the 'twenties was a one-pipe steam job of the all-on, all-off type. Hot water was not considered practical in tall buildings because the hydrostatic pressure mounted as stories were added and soon exceeded the design limits of the boiler. The room temperature was controlled by simply opening and closing windows when the system was "all on," and by hammering on the steam pipes when the system was "all off." Boilers and radiators were generously sized to avoid complaints.

When two- and three-story "garden type" apartments began to be built, hot water systems were a practical type to use. (Hydrostatic pressures were within the limits of low pressure boilers.) The chief advantage was the temperature control provided by modulating the hot water supply. A "one-pipe" hot water system could be installed at a cost not much more than that for steam.

The principle of modulating hot water, or even steam, was not new.

Modulation of steam had been proposed by some progressive manufacturers and had been used in a number of more elaborate projects where the higher cost of high-vacuum pumps and appurtenances could be justified. But for the lower cost garden apartment typical of the 'thirties, hot water was just as good as modulated steam and quite a bit cheaper.

Although hot water systems were restricted essentially to three-story jobs (when all equipment was located in the basement), the need for strict economy in the multi-story project required a tight control over the cost of heating, and the "open window" method of temperature control couldn't be tolerated. It was in this type of job that the newer developments in modulated steam and vapor systems were applicable. Simplified distribution piping and continuous down-feed radiation offset much of the cost of the differential pumps required to operate vapor systems at subatmospheric pressures.

Hot water systems are feasible in high buildings and have been used more recently simply by installing efficient heat exchangers in the upper levels. With

Individual room heaters   **Ductless (overflow)**   **Central heat ducted or piped to registers or radiators**

Three types of heating systems used in single-family houses which might be profitably adapted for use in multi-story apartments

*This article is based on a progress report on Housing and Home Finance Agency's Research Project No. 1-T-99 conducted under contract by Illinois Institute of Technology, Prof. E. I. Fiesenheiser, Project Director, Howard T. Fisher & Associates, Inc., Architects and Industrial Designers, Subcontractor. The substance of this research is dedicated to the public. The accuracy of all statements or interpretations is solely the responsibility of the author. Statements may be altered by further investigation.

automatically fired boilers, it is also possible to locate the heat generating equipment in an intermediate story or on the roof.

"Overdesign" Can Make Central Systems Costly

The biggest hitch with central heating systems is that the equipment is expensive, but generally it is more durable, not susceptible to tenant "tinkering," and designed for a long term investment. Some costs are not always justifiable, as the heating system may be overdesigned: for example, controls are installed to translate the effect of wind and sunshine into temperature of the water, the design is too greatly refined, and materials are more durable than obsolescence requires.

There has been great improvement in automatic controls, especially those which modulate the temperature of the heating medium according to outside weather conditions. In fact, that improvement seems to have been carried to excess. Ideally, a control should limit the amount of heat delivered to the apartment to that required to maintain 70 F with the windows closed. The individual room radiators or convectors should be easily controllable by the tenant so that he can shut them off to cool an individual room, rather than open the window. The main point is that the central system *can be designed* to produce a satisfactory result in terms of both comfort and economy.

Designers of heating systems for apartments often are not familiar with the developments in heating for individual single-family houses. Some of the ideas now widely used for single-family house heating, and quite adaptable to apartment heating, are neglected for no better reason than that they may be considered too elementary. The need for exchange of ideas is apparent.

Some Pros and Cons of Individual Heating

The use of individual heating units, either as room heaters or small systems similar to those used in single-family dwellings and supplied with fuel at the tenant's expense, has been proposed from time to time for apartment heating. (There may be some confusion between "individual heating" and "individual metering." Although individual metering implies individual heating, it would be possible to have individual meters on a central steam or hot water system.)

The study which follows, based on an investigation made by the St. Louis Housing Authority, indicates potential savings from individual heating *without* individual metering. There is a difference of opinion as to whether individual metering would result in added savings and whether these savings are socially justified.

The proposed use of individual heating systems in high buildings is relatively novel. Their actual use requires a re-orientation of some ideas fairly basic to the apartment vs. single-family-house types of living.

One of the reasons why people live in apartments is the economic one which motivates people to try to reduce their expenses by sharing them with others, the cost of heating by a central system, for example. Given equal living space and equally heat-resistant construction, it is obviously cheaper to heat that space which is in direct contact with other similar spaces than if it is in a separate shell of its own. And, usually, it is cheaper per heat unit to buy fuel in the large quantities required for an apartment house than the small quantities for single-family houses.

With individual heating, each tenant has the responsibility to keep his own apartment warm and not "borrow" heat from his neighbor. This situation is avoided when heat is paid for as part of the rent. There is some advantage to knowing in advance what the monthly costs of shelter will be and to spread the cost of heating over 12 months instead of over just the heating season.

There is also the health angle to be considered. In low rent housing, there is a social responsibility in protecting the welfare of the tenant. If he has his own heater, he may economize on fuel to an extent detrimental to his family's health.

These points favor central heating; other points are its proved acceptability,

predictable behavior, known costs, and durability. The proponents of individual heating stress the lower initial cost and opportunities to eliminate heat waste as the principal advantages.

Study of Individual Heating in St. Louis

A comparative study of four types of heating made for the St. Louis Housing Authority indicated a 33 per cent saving in combined operating and carrying charges for heating and domestic hot water produced by individual systems, as compared with a central steam system (see breakdown of charges, p. 32).

In the St. Louis study, gas was selected as the fuel for individual systems, and gas and oil for the central system. The individual heating systems are assumed to provide the same amount of heat and comfort as is provided with the radiator system. The fuel cost for the individual system is assumed to be eight per cent less than the central system, due to the elimination of transmission losses between boiler and radiator.

The principal savings are due to reduced cost of equipment and installation as reflected in carrying charges. Reduced labor for operation accounts for about one-third of the saving. Savings estimated for St. Louis are on a system *not having individual gas meters*.

With individual meters, tenants will not waste hot water or heat. These savings are important, since heating frequently represents the largest single item of operating cost, and in subsidized housing may amount to 35 or 40 per cent of the rent charged. It is possible that this might be offset by gas rates higher than those for bulk purchase. Submetering, if permitted, might eliminate this objection.

Potentialities of Gas Heating

Gas as fuel is not economical in all locations, but the extension of pipe lines

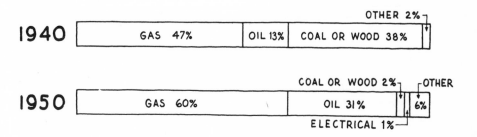

Types of fuel used for heating, classified as percentages of the total new homes built in 1940 and 1950. (Source: HHFA-RP-No. 129)

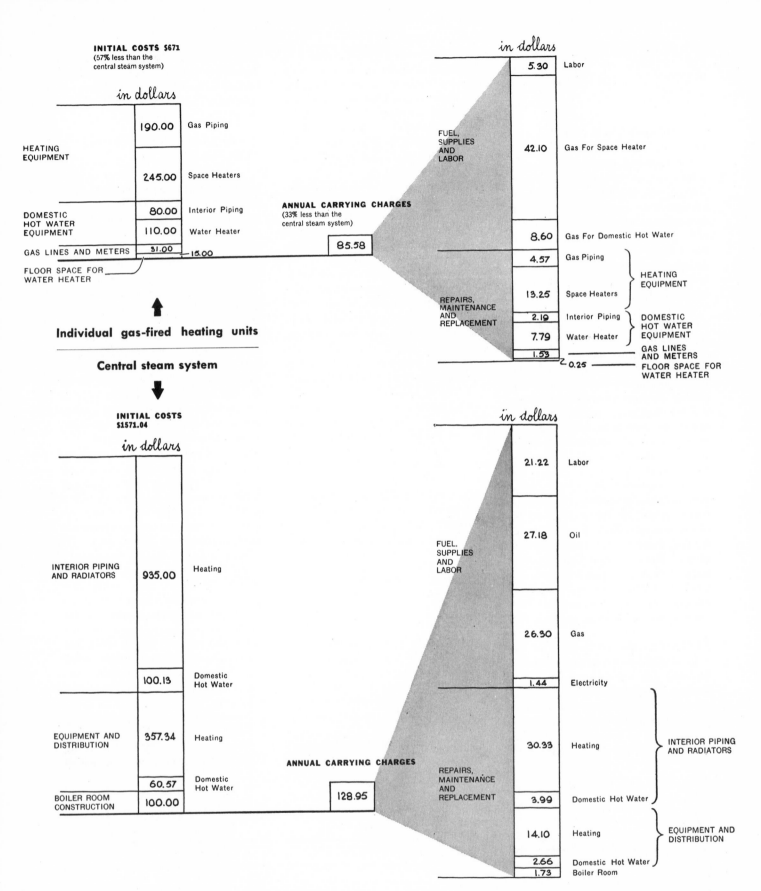

INITIAL COSTS $671
(57% less than the
central steam system)

in dollars

HEATING EQUIPMENT	190.00	Gas Piping
	245.00	Space Heaters
DOMESTIC HOT WATER EQUIPMENT	80.00	Interior Piping
	110.00	Water Heater
GAS LINES AND METERS	31.00	15.00

FLOOR SPACE FOR WATER HEATER

ANNUAL CARRYING CHARGES
(33% less than the
central steam system)

85.58

in dollars

FUEL, SUPPLIES AND LABOR	5.30	Labor
	42.10	Gas For Space Heater
	8.60	Gas For Domestic Hot Water
REPAIRS, MAINTENANCE AND REPLACEMENT	4.57	Gas Piping
	13.25	Space Heaters
	2.19	Interior Piping
	7.79	Water Heater
	1.53	

HEATING EQUIPMENT
DOMESTIC HOT WATER EQUIPMENT
GAS LINES AND METERS
0.25 — FLOOR SPACE FOR WATER HEATER

↑

Individual gas-fired heating units

Central steam system

↓

INITIAL COSTS
$1571.04

in dollars

INTERIOR PIPING AND RADIATORS	935.00	Heating
	100.13	Domestic Hot Water
EQUIPMENT AND DISTRIBUTION	357.34	Heating
	60.57	Domestic Hot Water
BOILER ROOM CONSTRUCTION	100.00	

ANNUAL CARRYING CHARGES

128.95

in dollars

FUEL, SUPPLIES AND LABOR	21.22	Labor
	27.18	Oil
	26.30	Gas
	1.44	Electricity
REPAIRS, MAINTENANCE AND REPLACEMENT	30.33	Heating
	3.99	Domestic Hot Water
	14.10	Heating
	2.66	Domestic Hot Water
	1.73	Boiler Room

INTERIOR PIPING AND RADIATORS
EQUIPMENT AND DISTRIBUTION

This study of the cost of heating and domestic water heating for high-rise apartments was made by George Hellmuth Associates, architects, and John D. Falvey, consulting engineer for the St. Louis Housing Authority. It shows a comparative analysis between a central steam system with gas-and-oil fired boilers serving 400-500 dwelling units each, and a system of individual gas-fired units for each apartment. The system with individual units, consisting of separate heaters for each room except kitchen and bath, was the first choice but had to be temporarily ruled out because gas was not available. The steam system analyzed in the cost breakdown was the second choice. Two other heating systems were also considered from natural gas regions, together with rises in cost of coal and oil, have resulted in a considerable increase in recent years in the use of gas for heating. The graph on page 32 shows the change from coal to gas from 1940 to 1950. Most of this increased use of gas has been in regions previously served largely by coal.

The increased use of insulation, together with the reduction in the size of single-family dwellings, has had an important effect on the type and size of heaters marketed and the fuel used; the size of heaters has decreased from a range of 120,000–70,000 Btu to 70,000–40,000 Btu. Heaters for apartments will drop these requirements to the 40,000–20,000 Btu bracket.

The reduction is possible because, with apartments above, below, and on both sides (except for corner apartments and the top floor), the surfaces through which heat is lost are reduced from six to two, and the large heat loss through the roof is eliminated.

With reduction in size and heat required per apartment, individual heating systems can be smaller, and fuel not practical previously may become the most economical to use.

It is obvious that all systems will not give the same degree of comfort, nor cost the same. The degree of refinement of the heating system should be related to the rental level of the particular project. When this factor is overlooked, the result is often a system too costly for a low rental project or one that lacks the refinements required by tenants in a higher rental project.

Four Heating Types

In this article we will consider four basically different types of individual heating. These are outlined here as applied to the typical apartment plan shown on page 22.

1: Single Overflow Heater per apartment. (The term "Overflow Heater" indicates one that heats more than one room by flow of warm air through open doors without the aid of ducts.) The logical location for a single heater system would be the center of the dwelling, or as close to it as possible. This heater can operate on gravity or fan for circulation. Bureau of Standards tests in a one-story bungalow indicated that although the use of the fan changed the pattern of heat distribution, there was not very much difference in comfort.

Because of the central location of the heater, a vertical vent will be most practical.

2: Separate Space Heaters *located in each bedroom and living room under the windows and vented horizontally direct to the outside air.* This gives a better distribution of heat than Type 1. A heater would not be needed in the kitchen because, normally, the heat from cooking would keep this room warm. It would be desirable, though, to have a register opening between living room and kitchen, possibly incorporating a fan so that heat may be supplied to the kitchen when necessary.

Since air leaves the apartment through a power vent in the bathroom, warm air from the apartment will be drawn to this room; in some cases, a radiator may be connected with the hot water supply for the bathroom.

3: Warm Air Duct System. This combines the merit of warm air discharge under the windows with the economy of one central heater. There are two principal ways in which the air can be dis-

Required size of space heaters has changed

The old-fashioned house without insulation required a large-capacity furnace

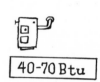

70-125 Btu

A modern well-insulated house does not require such large equipment

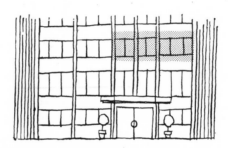

40-70 Btu

And a single apartment would require a still smaller unit

20-40 Btu

1. Single Overflow Heater

2. Separate Space Heater

33

tributed: by gravity, with the heater located on the floor below the apartment to be heated; or by forced circulation, with the heater within the apartment to be heated and with registers at floor or ceiling level.

For maintenance of the gravity system, there must be access to the heating unit through the apartment below, but in a rental project, this should offer no serious difficulty. On the other hand, the forced system would have higher installation and maintenance costs.

The air can be heated by a separate hot air heater or by connecting a heat exchanger with the domestic hot water heater, which would perform the dual function of providing hot air and domestic hot water.

4: Radiators heated by Domestic Hot Water System. If the domestic hot water heater is to be the source of heat for the apartment, it may be more economical to place the heat exchangers right in the rooms in the form of hot water radiators and to run a pipe system to them, rather than to have a heat exchanger heating the air to be carried to the rooms by ducts. The decision will depend to some extent on the type of floor system used. If the floor system provides spaces within it which can be used as ducts, the central heat exchanger may be more economical, but if the floor and ceiling system is not suitable as a duct system, it may be more economical to use pipes and radiators.

When the hot water heater is used for this dual purpose, it is advisable to have a 40- or 45-gallon storage tank instead of the 30-gallon tank used for domestic hot water alone, and the capacity of the heater ought to be about 45,000 Btu/hr. The cost of this type of system should be lower than that of the individual domestic hot water heater plus a space heater. It is absolutely essential, if the domestic hot water heater is also used for space heating, that the tank and radiators be made of noncorroding materials. A galvanized tank will rust when used for heating as well as hot water because the water temperatures will frequently be higher than when used for domestic hot water only, and galvanizing is not likely to stand up. Where there are appreciable quantities of lime in the water, a central water treatment apparatus should be installed to eliminate the lime.

The design of the system and the selection of equipment should be such that the combined cost is less than that of a central plant supplying both heat

Two ways of heating air

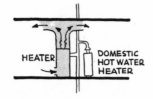

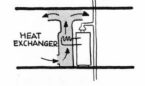

Space heater

Heat-exchanger with hot water coils
from domestic water boiler

3. Warm Air Duct System

Three ways of distributing warm air

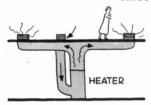

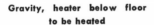

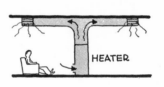

Gravity, heater below floor
to be heated

Forced air, ducts at ceiling

Forced air, ducts under floor

Two types of hot water heating

4. Radiators

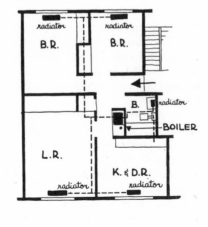

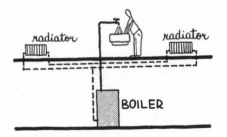

Gravity, boiler below floor to be heated

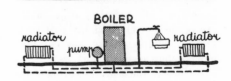

Forced, boiler within the apartment to be heated

and hot water. Durability of equipment also has an effect on overall cost.

Labor Costs

Labor costs for operation will probably be quite a bit lower with individual heating plants. This is particularly true in certain localities where union regulations and codes require that licensed operators of certain qualifications be employed to run a central heating system, even though the system may be designed and installed so as to eliminate the need for most attention.

In Chicago, for example, the cost of such personnel would average $5200 per man per year. Three men (for three shifts) will be required to service a central plant for 300 apartments. Labor costs will vary with local codes, type of fuel, type of heating equipment, and size of project. The estimated labor cost in St. Louis for operating and servicing a central heating plant supplying 400 apartments (see page 33) is estimated at $21.22 per apartment per year. In Chicago, the labor cost for the same size project (assuming four men required) would be approximately $52 per apartment. Such costs should not be considered a valid reason for shifting to individual heating systems. This is a matter for the local citizenry to deal with through changes in legislation, but, still, as long as such conditions exist, they cannot be ignored by the budget-minded housing executive.

Comfort Factors

Individually heated apartments can be more comfortable than those heated by a central system. There are several reasons why this may be so. With a central heating system, the hours that heat is supplied may not meet the time schedule of all families. If a central hot water radiator system with modulated controls is used, it will frequently be found that the system is not responsive to requirements of all rooms since there are bound to be variations in exposure to wind and sun.

The central heating system, though, has become such an established symbol of comfort and housing progress that a return to individual heating systems, although refined by modern technology, may be slow in receiving general acceptance. It is often argued that the performance of individual apartment heating systems is inferior to central systems. This is due to the association of individual heating systems with the single centrally located overflow heater, which, obviously, cannot give as good distribution of heat as a unit in each room.

If heating units — be they space heaters, registers or radiators — are provided in each room adjacent to the windows, there should be slight, if any, difference in the pattern of heat distribution, no matter if the units are activated by an individual or by a central plant. Since there is little difference in comfort — with the exception of the overflow heating system — the question then becomes one largely of economics.

Economics

The economy of individual systems has many aspects. The St. Louis cost analysis shows a lower cost for individual heating in comparison with central heating. This is due largely to lower carrying charges because of lower initial cost. In the St. Louis Housing Project, there is a central gas meter, and the same amount of heat per apartment has been figured as with the central plant.

The unit cost of gas to the tenant, even if the gas is purchased wholesale and submetered by the landlord, will necessarily be higher than with a central meter since there would have to be carrying charges on the meters and additional bookkeeping and collection costs. Whether this higher unit cost will be counterbalanced by the opportunity for savings which the tenant has by reducing waste (and maybe comfort), is an open question that may depend on rate structure, climate, type of building, location of the apartment in the building, and consumer habits.

Another facet in the heating cost to the tenant, a psychological one, is the fact that tenants have come to expect heating supplied "free" by the landlord (included in the rent).

Comfort With Overflow Heaters

Where economy is paramount or climate is mild, overflow heaters may be found adequate for low-cost housing. With 48.2 per cent* of all homes in the United States heated with space heaters, there may be justification for the opinion that a comfort condition acceptable for those Americans who pay for their own homes should be high enough for those who live in subsidized housing.

---

* U. S. Bureau of Census — 1950 Census of Housing.

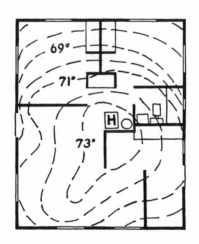

Heat distribution in a single-family house*

* From a study made in 1940–41 by I. M. Moriyama, under the direction of the Sub-Committee on the Hygiene of Housing, American Public Health Association

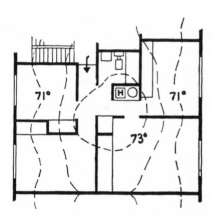

Assumed heat distribution in a multi-story apartment, 4 ft above the floor

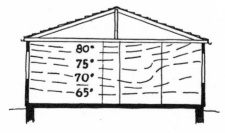

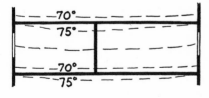

Heat distribution should be better in apartments than in single-family houses. In a single-family house, the greatest heat loss is through the roof. Also, overflow heaters in houses do not adequately eliminate cold floors. In an apartment, surrounded by other heated apartments, heat loss through the ceiling is largely eliminated, and the floors are warm

It can be argued that an overflow heater should give more comfortable heat distribution in an apartment than in a single-family dwelling of comparable size and floor plan.

While the exposure is less in an apartment dwelling unit than in a single-family residence, the windows which might occur in two walls of one room in a residence, may be combined in an apartment into one big window. This may cause a reverse circulation of air cooled by the glass, and set up uncomfortable air currents across the floor. The effectiveness of overflow heaters depends upon the compactness of the plan, the distance between interconnecting rooms, the total load to be handled in relation to the heat loss of the space in which the heater is located, and the heat losses of the individual rooms adjoining the heater room. In other words, the house or apartment must be small, compact, and of low heat loss.

The FHA, in specifying the conditions under which overflow heating is acceptable, limits the distance between the center of the heater outlet and the center of any room heated by the overflow heater to 18 ft, limits its use to dwellings having a calculated heat loss of 45,000 Btu or less, and prescribes not more than one doorway and one arched opening between the heater and the adjacent rooms.

Flues for Venting Gas-Fired Equipment

In the minds of most people, venting is still considered a serious obstacle to the use of individual heating in high-rise apartments. This is largely due to lack of information and experience on the vertical venting of individual gas equipment located on each floor. The American Gas Association, as a result of our research project, is conducting an investigation of this problem and expects to develop authoritative data for the design of individual and/or common vents.

The problem in tall buildings is not that of getting enough draft, but rather of preventing too much draft under certain conditions. Gas equipment operates on a very low negative chimney pressure, and since chimney draft varies with height, the average chimney temperature and the high stacks necessary in tall buildings are the most important problems. Assuming that the effect of excessive height can be overcome by lowering the gas temperatures, there is a serious problem of dealing with con-

densation, which, with fuel gas, occurs in the stack at temperatures of around 140 F.

One possible solution would be to design the vent as three independent vents, each three stories in height. The admittance of air at every third floor would prevent over-draft due to height of the building. This design is being considered by the American Gas Association as part of its study.

In buildings three or four stories in height, individual vents are often used. At first thought, one would assume that individual vents would take a great deal of space in a ten-story building, but since the individual aluminum vents need be only 4 in. in diameter, it is entirely possible to provide ten vents in a space 8 by 26 in., which is very little more space than required by a common vent. Since the vents can be constructed of .013 in. aluminum, the cost is nominal.

There is, however, a system suitable for immediate application, which has already been accepted by a number of building codes. This consists of a horizontal vent direct to the outside air for each individual heating unit. (This is the system that was intended for the St. Louis Housing Authority 7-story apartment. Also, the Los Angeles Housing Authority has plans for a 13-story building using this system.)

Availability of Fuels

A limiting factor in many communities at this time is the availability of gas for residential heating. The St. Louis Housing Authority would have used individual gas heaters if gas had been available. Availability is dependent on supply *and* storage. Since peak heating loads may be only for short periods during the heating season, the facilities for storage may be a more important factor than production capacity or pipe lines. This situation is being rapidly altered.

A project is under way in the Chicago area for storing gas in a natural underground dome of porous sandstone. This will have the effect of trebling the capacity to meet peak loads in this area.

One of the largest distributors of natural gas is putting in storage and pipe lines, in order to meet their anticipated residential demand.

However, considering the potential economies which research so far has demonstrated, it seems certain that the next few years will see a wide use in apartment houses of heating methods which were formerly considered practical only for single-family homes.

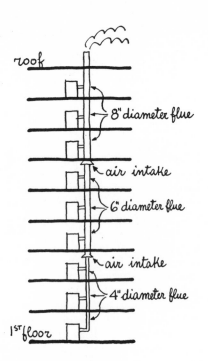

Common flue for gas space heaters in high-rise apartments. This is a proposed design with air intakes every third floor to prevent excessive draft

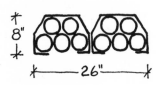

Individual flues can be easily nested to save space. Ten single 4-in. flues—sufficient for individual heaters in a ten-story building—occupy only 1.44 sq ft

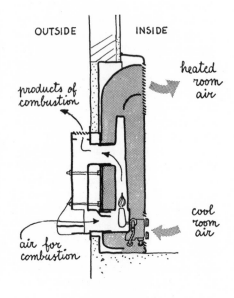

This individual gas room heater is vented directly through the outside wall

II *Apartments:*
Community-Scale Projects

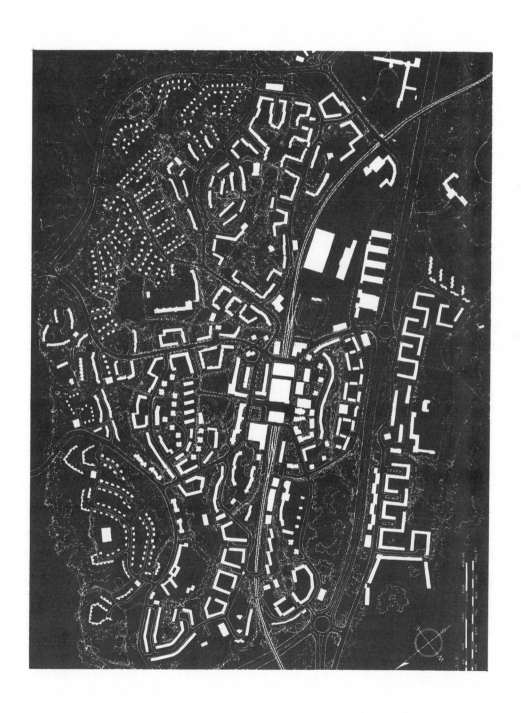

COMMUNITIES FOR THE GOOD LIFE

By Clarence S. Stein *

THE GOOD LIFE! Never before have so many people had so much time to enjoy a good life. But with what feeble results! The trouble is that there are so many buildings and highways all jammed together that there is not space to enjoy our opportunities. The 20th century technological revolution makes possible — in fact, it demands — leisure for all. This is in complete contrast to the 19th century industrial revolution which glorified labor and crowded its slum dwellings tight around its temples of industry.

In the movie "A Nous la Liberte" Rene Clair foretold this change 25 years ago. He showed the schoolroom of the 19th century with children taught as though it were a religion — "One *must* work." Adults who loafed were jailed, while those who labored did so in jail-like factories. And then mechanization took command. Ultimately it produced without human aid. Man at last had realized his fondest ambition — freedom from drudgery. And what did the workers do with their permanent holiday? In "A Nous la Liberte" everyone went fishing or dancing. Rene Clair a quarter of a century ago wrote this as a fantastic wish — like Jules Verne's tales. And now it is being realized. For the first time in man's history there is leisure — an ever-increasing leisure for more and more people — here in America. And there is every prospect that it is going to increase immeasurably.

Never before has the world or its architects been faced with this problem. Leisure, yes; but it has been leisure of the selected few: Hadrian's Villa, Versailles, hunting enclosures, the Riviera. The architect — you and I — face the task of setting the stage for a completely new production.

Leisure occupations for all require above all SPACE, much open space, convenient open space, verdant space. And the whole landscape has been cluttered with crowded, unrelated disorder. We are hemmed in by dangerous, nerve-wracking motor-ways. Open green places are engulfed and destroyed as the obsolete city pattern rolls out. Much of the time we have gained by shorter working hours and longer weekends is squandered in tiresome, jerky journeys in search of open spaces. Fields and woods and wilderness grow constantly

more distant, as more and more open countryside is bulldozed into dreary checkerboard monotony. No matter how many billions are spent on our new thoroughway program, it cannot keep up with the increasing problem of more people going further and further to find less and less space.

So before our highway engineers flood most of our landscape under a sea of pavement, we architects must develop a saner plan for using leisure. We must bring the peaceful quiet and the beauty and the sense of great openness into every part of all our communities, as near as possible to where people live and work. Just outside everyone's own private garden or balcony there must be spacious open commons; plentiful green places attractive for leisurely loafing in the sun, or under a great tree, with lots of room for children to play freely and safely near home. Above all we need flexible space that can be used for various purposes as the neighbors get new ideas of how to spend their spare time, together or by themselves. Not in just playing games or sitting around talking and thinking, but in constructive action such as building a little community workshop or a nursery.

A moderate sized well-designed area can give a sense of spaciousness and of mysterious distance just beyond the corner. This is apparent in the exquisite gardens in Soochow, China, and in those of Japan. Here in America in a quite different way Thomas Church is making much of little, as Marjorie Cautlie did for me at Radburn and elsewhere. For utility as well as beauty open spaces are the basic element of design. Chinese artists and philosophers have long recognized this. Twenty-five hundred years ago Lao-Tzu said, "Clay is moulded into a vessel; the utility of the vessel depends on the hollow interior." To permanently augment the value of houses, group them around an attractive empty space. Harmony and melody, essential to the good life, dwell in spaciousness, not in congestion. Great Chinese painters composed the empty areas so that they delighted the soul even more than the subject of their pictures. And so, we are coming to understand that the all embracing view is more essential to good living than the finest interior.

For peaceful living the open spaces on which all houses face must be insulated from the racket, the odors, the deathly danger of through traffic ways. Therefore

*Paper presented by Mr. Stein at the annual dinner of the American Institute of Architects' convention in Los Angeles in 1956, when he was awarded the Institute's Gold Medal.

Copyright 1956 by F. W. Dodge Corporation

they should be built into the center of the blocks, separated from the highways. At the same time the homes and other buildings that surround them must be directly accessible to motor machines.

This kind of practical modern planning is possible only if we completely eliminate the conventional street layout and build a framework and substance that grows out of our needs of both living a leisurely life and being in convenient touch with work places and stores. The heart and arterial system is the tranquil chain of parks toward which the buildings face and through which the local life of the community flows. The highways become servants, not masters, of the community life. The main streams of traffic flow as freely and steadily as on a parkway or throughway. Buildings and grounds open only on subordinate roads. All parking is off street parking.

This means that homes and other structures face in two directions at the same time, one toward peaceful green spaciousness, and the other toward roads and services. Thus there are two separate frameworks for the modern communities. One is for motors, the other for pedestrians. The one is gray, the other green. They fit together like the fingers of two hands, but they never overlap or interfere with each other's functions.

In the contemporary city the green openness will go far beyond the built-in-parks, flowing through and connecting the super-blocks. Not only will every building open on views of fine old trees or distant hills, but broad green belts will be close by for agriculture or forests, for great sport fields or hiking, boating, fishing, swimming, skating, or just for solitude in the peaceful valleys or the wilds.

This is the kind of beautiful and healthful city that can be built in various parts of the United States if we start from the ground up. When they are seen and lived in I am sure that those who remain in the archaic cities will insist that redevelopment must also start from the ground up; that is must also clear away all signs of the 19th century pattern. Thus we can build truly green modern cities on the sites of the old stony deserts. The regional cities which are destined to replace our mad metropolitan monstrosities will consist of a constellation of such moderate-sized communities set against a great green background of fields, forests and wilderness.

Such communities cannot be secured by the ordinary piece-meal process of city planning. A beautiful and livable urban environment cannot be boxed into cubbyholes bounded by fixed and dominating streets and lot lines. It must be created as an entity, embracing the site, the mass of buildings and their relation to each other and to the natural setting; in short, to all the visual surroundings.

You may say that this is not a problem of architecture, it is a question of securing adequate land and planning it for leisure-time use where it is needed. But the fact is, the two must go hand in hand, the design of building and outdoor spaces for the new life and the allocation of adequate and proper land where and when it is needed.

The architect must take the leadership in this job. For it *is* architecture, but architecture in a broader and ever-broadening field.

What we need is an architectural attack on problems much more comprehensive than the individual building. The architect must deal with the whole environment in which his building is an essential, harmonious part — and without which the architect's work is impotent. The community may merely be a small group of interdependent structures, it may — most likely will be — a neighborhood, an urban district, a whole town or city, or even a region.

The procedure of a community architect parallels the practice of realistic contemporary architectural offices. This is illustrated by the design of a high school, which has many community relations similar to those of a small community. These include a campus free of auto traffic, surrounded by inter-related buildings both for families or classes and for community assembly, recreation, work, dining, administration. Interiors open on out-door-rooms and courts. There are even schools within schools just as there are communities within neighborhoods, neighborhoods within towns, towns within regional cities. In the creation of a community, as of a school, the effective architect actively participates in the whole process of development from conception to realization. In association with the municipal administrator he coordinates the functional, operational and physical requirements of the expert practitioners in many fields. This so that his design will properly relate, harmonize and translate them into a unified structural entity that will be thoroughly practical and pleasing. Thus a town is created that works efficiently, effectively, and economically from the beginning, as a setting for good living — good modern living.

The architect in the new and changing world must accept this broader field of architectural practice because only so can he protect the buildings he creates. Their appearance is dependent far more on their setting than on their mass or the design of their facades. Their usefulness is limited by surrounding structures — and even more by the movement of traffic in the streets. The most efficient steady flow of material through an industrial plant can be completely negated by blocked traffic outside its doors. The causes of the congestion, decay, blight that surround your work may have its roots in defective, obsolete arrangement of highways and structures many miles away. And so, if only for self-setting — and city — and region in which his contemporary building can play its modern role. But the primary reason why all of us must parallel our practice as architects of buildings with the broader practice of community architecture is less selfish than this. It is because America's greatest peace need is modern cities — cities that really work, that bear a sane and constructive relation to living here and now.

Many such cities must be built here if America is to hold its leadership among modern progressive nations. The architectural profession must fill the same position in design of modern cities as it has in design of buildings. It is a duty — but a very pleasant one — a field for adventure, exploration, discovery — glorious attainments.

Note that I suggest COMMUNITY ARCHITECTURE, not CITY PLANNING, as a fitting, an essential practice for our profession. The two fields are basically different.

City planning deals with two-dimensional diagramming, with a city's framework for circulation, and its subdivision into block and lots. Its specifications are negative regulations and generalized limitations, such as zoning. They are not positive, specific, constructive requirements as those for a particular building. Thus the detailed form and mass of a city is not designed, but is merely limited.

I recognize and admire the able public-spirited work that city planning administrators are doing. It is essential under present limitations, but these make it impossible to accomplish the purpose of the constructive rebuilding of America that we need so badly. For what is called city planning does not create solid realities; it outlines phantom cities. It does not determine the bulk, the solid body of a city. It is not positive, creative, as is architecture. It produces skeletons, framework for marketable lots, not vibrant communities of homes and working places for realistic and pleasant living and doing here and now in the 20th century. The ultimate shape and appearance of these cities is a chaotic accident. It is the summation of the haphazard, antagonistic whims of many self-centered, ill-advised individuals. Under these conditions people have little freedom of choice. They can fit their building into one of the cubbyholes outlined by a plot plan, or fit their family's life into the monotonous repetitive patterns stamped out by the builders machine. Look at Los Angeles!

It shows, as do most American metropolitan areas that the only way to get modern cities and to keep them modern is by all inclusive architecturally planned city building, followed by permanent dynamic administration to keep their purpose and form alive.

That zoning or similar restrictive methods will not serve this purpose is apparent in the present development of the San Fernando Valley. The City Planning Department of Los Angeles made a far sighted plan to prevent the continuous sprawl of population over the 212 square miles of the Valley. They separated the moderate sized communities from each other by green belts zoned as agricultural open areas. This has come to naught. For the practical house developers have had the green belts erased where most needed, that is between the growing communities. Zoning is only a temporary barrier or protection. It cannot stand up against the

flood of monotonous commonplace or the greed of land subdividers. To permanently preserve green belts and keep modern green towns green and modern requires constructive, purposeful development and operation. Positive action must replace negative regulation for cities as well as buildings. That is why I am convinced that architects must be community architects.

In the development of a new culture, certain physical expressions of a civilization are affected much more slowly by technical, social and economic change. For example our cities have lagged far behind our buildings. The Technological Revolution has given us a fresh contemporary architecture. Look at our schools, our hospitals, our factories. They reflect a new way of living and doing, new understanding, new conceptions. The architects of America are beginning to develop an architecture that is thoroughly contemporary. We may even be on the threshold of a golden period of American architecture. Architects are free to mold and model their works to express their purpose and their feeling.

But our architecture is by no means fully free, for in our cities our buildings have no where to go. The golden period of American architecture will have to wait until our lagging cities recognize that this is the mid-twentieth century.

Modern architecture demands a modern setting, a place where it can be properly viewed and enjoyed, a site where it can open up and stretch and change. As community architects we must create cities and buildings as a single entity, completely inter-related in design and structures. These new communities should remain continuously youthful. Therefore they must be both spacious and flexible enough to take new form with changing ways of living, laboring and loafing. We must replace dying cities with communities that fit and foster the activities and aspirations of the present time. We must build new cities as a stage — a joyful setting for the good life here and now.

VÄLLINGBY

THE NEW SECTION OF STOCKHOLM

By G. E. Kidder Smith

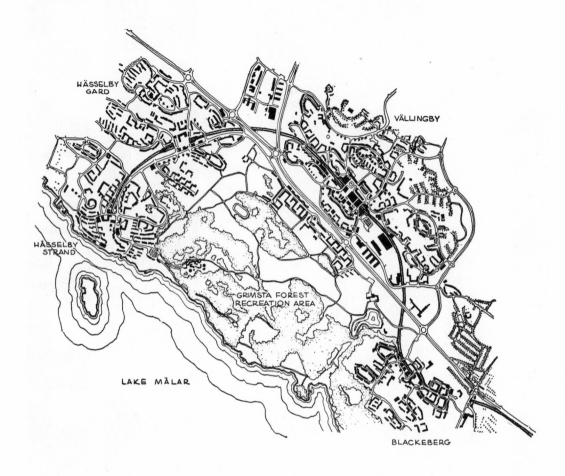

HÄSSELBY GARD

VÄLLINGBY

HÄSSELBY STRAND

GRIMSTA FOREST RECREATION AREA

LAKE MÄLAR

BLACKEBERG

VÄLLINGBY, the new town section in west Stockholm, probably has more planning lessons to offer the cities of our time than any recent urban development within my knowledge. By beautiful example, it shows how the suburbs which increasingly envelope the world's cities can be well planned, park-like, viable centers — not haphazard accretions strangled by transportation, mired in shopping, desperately in need of adequate schools and public amenity. Here, where cows grazed and corn grew only five short years ago, there is a city of 23,000 in which every road, every building location, every need of the inhabitants was carefully planned before first ground was ever broken. Vällingby is the embodiment of Sweden's intimate re-lationship between architecture and the land. Where has this idea been more beautifully expressed?

An expanded version of this article appears in a greatly revised 2nd edition of Sweden Builds, published in 1957 by Reinhold, New York. The photographic illustra-tions are by Mr. Smith

VIRTUALLY ALL the major decisions in the moulding of Vällingby were good ones: strict preservation of the landscape; free planning in space with fingers of green everywhere; separation of pedestrian and motor traffic; integrated transportation, parking and shopping; complete cultural and entertainment facilities; a great variety of housing types; one central plant for heat and power. One might quarrel with minor decisions — especially with some of the architecture — but the basic concept and its execution are decidedly superior. Why and how did Vällingby come about?

A few years ago further expansion of Stockholm was imperative. The City Planning Commission, under Sven Markelius' brilliant direction, decided that a complete town section — a microcosm of the city — would be sounder in principle than the usual dormitory suburb. They conceived Vällingby as an important experiment in character and in size. Its character was

set by the inclusion of a modified commercial and industrial base capable of employing 25 per cent of the resident population. Its size would exceed anything in Scandinavia. Indeed there are few new developments anywhere which can approach it in scope.

The site — nine miles from central Stockholm — comprised four square miles of unspoiled farmland which the city had foresightedly bought in 1930. In addition to accommodating its own 23,000 people, Vällingby was planned as the shopping, amusement and employment center for 60,000 additional people grouped in surrounding developments. Each of these would be intimately related to the large Grimsta Forest Recreation Area and to Lake Mälar, the southern border of the complex. The entire development is a magnificent concept as well as an effective demonstration of the foresight and virtues of Stockholm's municipal land ownership and large-scale planning.

SCALE:

50 100   200   300   400 M.

100   300   500   700   900   1100   1300 FT.

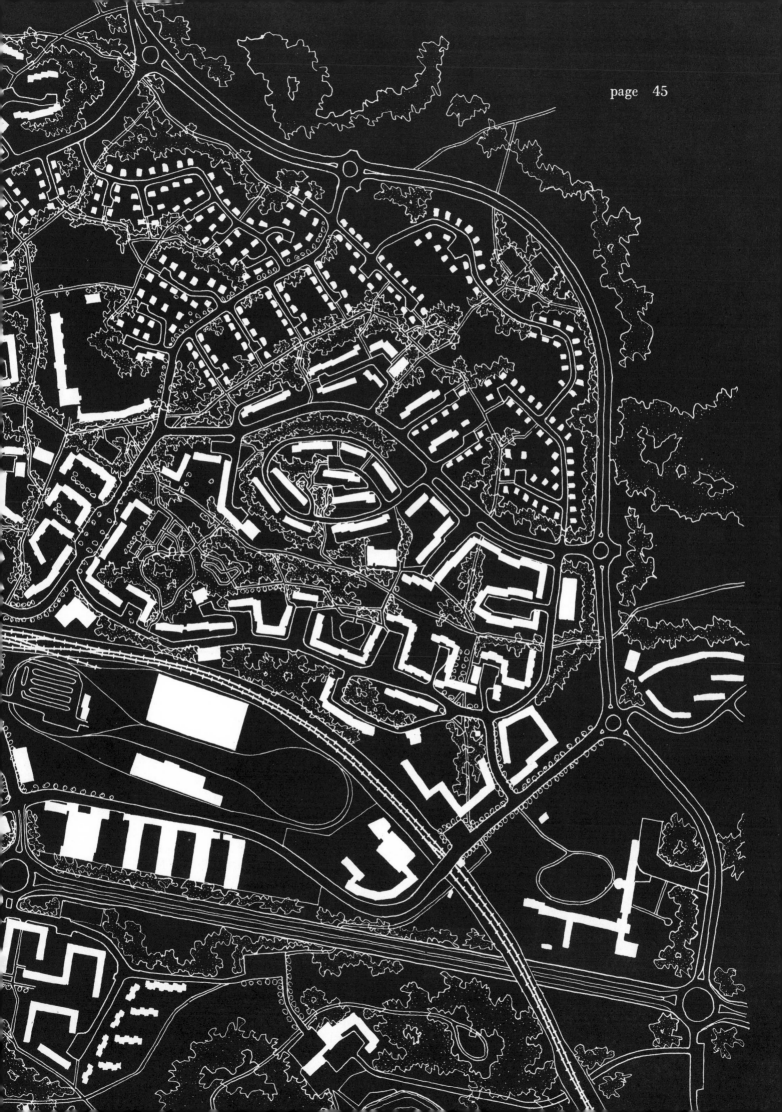

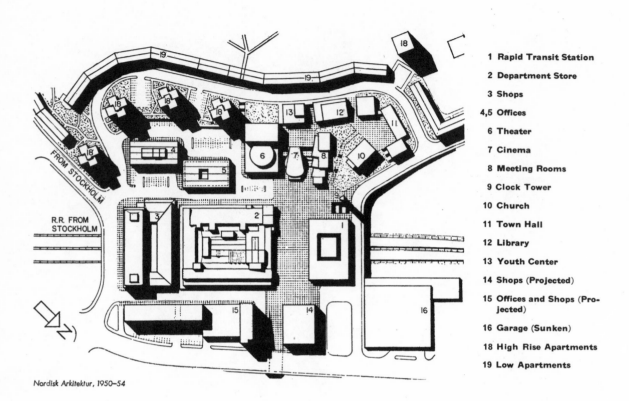

1 Rapid Transit Station

2 Department Store

3 Shops

4,5 Offices

6 Theater

7 Cinema

8 Meeting Rooms

9 Clock Tower

10 Church

11 Town Hall

12 Library

13 Youth Center

14 Shops (Projected)

15 Offices and Shops (Projected)

16 Garage (Sunken)

18 High Rise Apartments

19 Low Apartments

Nordisk Arkitektur, 1950–54

VÄLLINGBY / CENTRUM The core of Vällingby combines the commercial, amusement and cultural activities of the 80,000 people in the entire three-community development. It is built directly over the Rapid Transit Lines and is surrounded by parking. Deliveries and servicing for most of the seventy shops are from below. No vehicles are allowed on the piazza: the pedestrian rules here. Public buildings (most of which were designed by Backstrom and Reinius) are grouped along the slight hillside and step down to the main shopping mall. With its fountains, gay mosaic paving and rampant lamps, the mall is very festive, although the space is a bit rigid. Furthermore it is doubtful if the disposition of the major buildings gives enough weather protection in a latitude which bisects Siberia. The general atmosphere is stimulating and conducive to spending, despite the shockingly tasteless signs — typical of many Scandinavian commercial buildings.

VÄLLINGBY / HIGH RISE APARTMENTS In planning the community one of the basic decisions was to group a concentration of ten to twelve-story apartments about the centrum. As distance from the core increases, density and building height diminish. This places the greatest number of people near shopping and next to the rapid transit station. Special flats for older persons are appropriately located near the centrum. For families with children, who welcome intimate contact with nature, and for those with cars, walk-up apartments, row-houses and cottages are available farther out. An interesting feature of the Vällingby concept is the extraordinary variety of accommodation available: one can get anything from a twelfth floor penthouse to a prefabricated cottage. And no matter what the type each unit will be surrounded by greenery.

(H. Klemming was the architect for the buildings shown on these two pages.)

VÄLLINGBY / LOW HOUSING Three and sometimes four-story walk-up housing forms the major building type, but there is by no means a single pattern for this, as can be seen in the sketch above and photograph at upper right. Its finest expression is shown in the sketch and plan above (by Paul Hedqvist). These are well planned, spaciously deployed dwellings, intimate with the land. The three story strip (or lamella) housing is Vällingby's commonest type. Sometimes it is well designed (as at right, by H. Klemming), sometimes not—as in the dreary, clumsy southwest corner of the city (see plan, bottom of p. 44). Note—above right—that tree preservation, landscaping and playgrounds are integral with the architecture. Landscaping goes hand in hand with construction here, and is not treated as an afterthought with an afterthought's results. The attached houses at lower right are skillfully tied to their setting (by Höjer and Lundqvist).

BRAZIL: A NEW OCEANSIDE COMMUNITY

High Rise Apartments and Houses Integrated

Pernambuco Beach Development, Guarujá, Brazil

Henrique E. Mindlin, Architect

Marjory & Jorge Prado, Developer-owners

TWO-THIRDS of the population in this new community near Santos and 35 miles from São Paulo will live in high-rise apartment buildings, five of which will become a visual focus in the scheme. The design illustrates the architect's two-fold interest in achieving a careful organization of various buildings, open spaces and circulation for the most favorable sun, view, breeze and intercommunication — and in creating a pleasant environment for living. There was in addition a strong concern for preserving the native character of the site — a magnificent one-and-one-quarter mile stretch of beach facing east to the Atlantic and bounded on the west by a river, rugged hills and a wild forest.

The community plan calls for one through highway, located nearly 1000 ft from and parallel to the beach, creating two main areas. The part nearest the ocean is restricted solely to pedestrian traffic and is given over to gardens, beach clubs, hotels, apartments and houses. Toward the hills, a secondary loop-road feeds a larger segment containing a golf course, shooting club, polo field, tennis club and house-building plots. Note that traffic in all residential areas has been channelled into dead-end streets, thereby both restricting and slowing it. The relatively small amount of commercial activity centers about the traffic circle (far left in plan). It is significant that the completed project is to be 87 per cent green, 6 per cent buildings, 7 per cent roads.

Note particularly the plan for the development of the five large blocks fronting on the beach. Cul-de-sac roads feed the residential plots (shown white on the plan) which in turn open to a large common garden. The ten-story, 80 unit apartment buildings adjacent to the highway also face this garden and look over it to the sea. The land area between and about the pilotis for

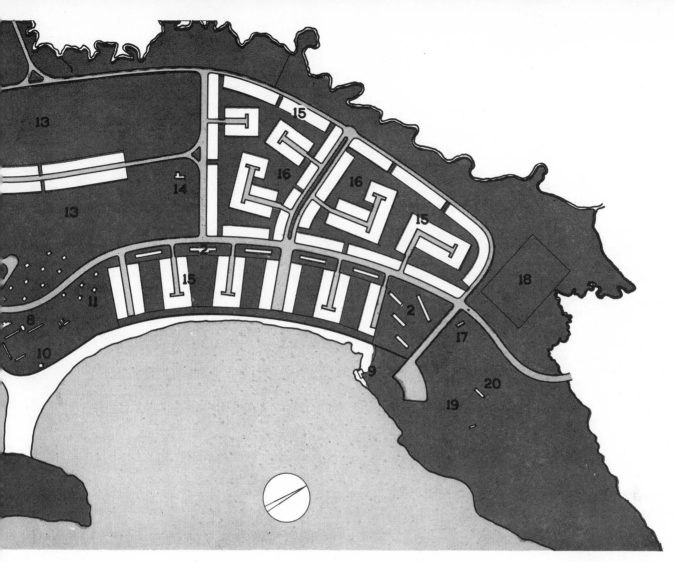

LEGEND

1. School
2. Apartment Building
3. Low Cost Rental Housing
4. Church
5. Commercial
6. Shopping Center
7. Community Center
8. Hotel
9. Beach Club
10. Pavilion
11. Cottages
12. Shooting Club
13. Golf Course
14. Golf Club House
15. Residential Lots
16. Tennis Courts
17. Tennis Club
18. Polo Grounds
19. Riding Course
20. Riding Club

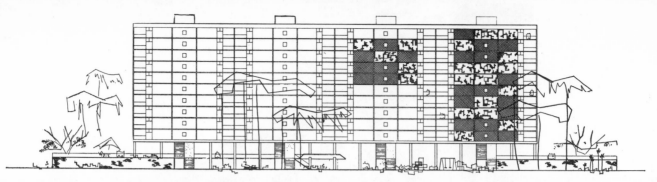

Elevation from the highway

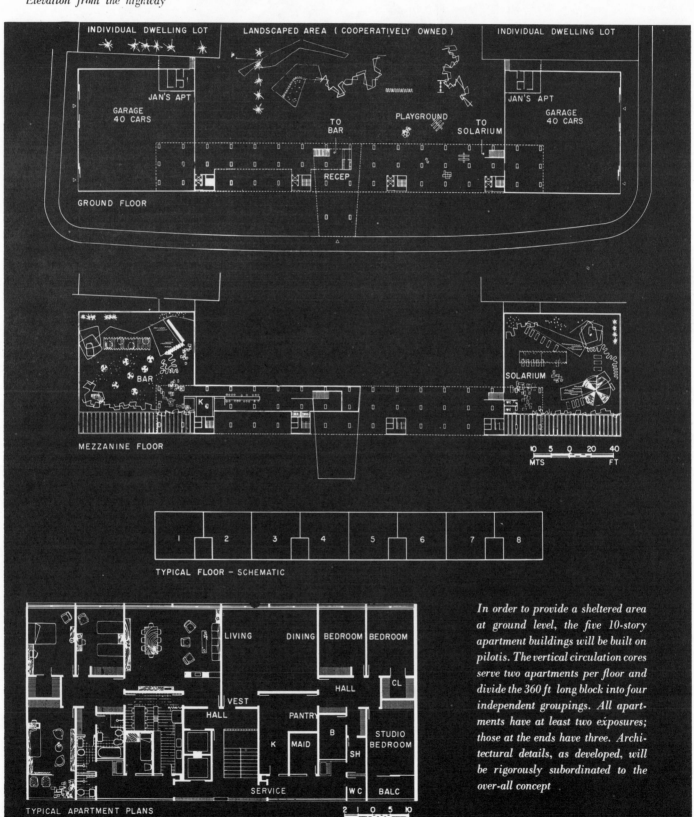

INDIVIDUAL DWELLING LOT   LANDSCAPED AREA (COOPERATIVELY OWNED)   INDIVIDUAL DWELLING LOT

JAN'S APT

GARAGE
40 CARS

TO BAR

PLAYGROUND

TO SOLARIUM

JAN'S APT

GARAGE
40 CARS

RECEP

GROUND FLOOR

BAR

K

SOLARIUM

MEZZANINE FLOOR

10 5 0 20 40
MTS   FT

1   2   3   4   5   6   7   8

TYPICAL FLOOR – SCHEMATIC

LIVING   DINING   BEDROOM   BEDROOM

HALL

CL

VEST

HALL   PANTRY

K   MAID   B

STUDIO
BEDROOM

SH

SERVICE

WC   BALC

TYPICAL APARTMENT PLANS

2 1 0 5 10
MTS   FT

In order to provide a sheltered area at ground level, the five 10-story apartment buildings will be built on pilotis. The vertical circulation cores serve two apartments per floor and divide the 360 ft long block into four independent groupings. All apartments have at least two exposures; those at the ends have three. Architectural details, as developed, will be rigorously subordinated to the over-all concept

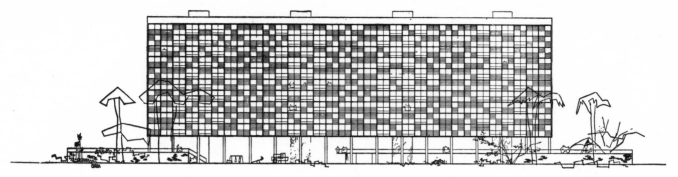

Elevation from the sea

each of these tall apartments is to be devoted to parking, gardens, and playgrounds, comprising a total area of approximately 90,000 sq ft. The individual plots for houses are small for two principal reasons: first, because each opens to the large communal park — second, to make for easier landscape maintenance.

The restrictions necessary in order to carry out the concept have been readily accepted by the individual lot owners. Everyone concerned seems to understand why the architecture must be modern, that certain required alignments are necessary, and that free spaces next to individual lots must be preserved.

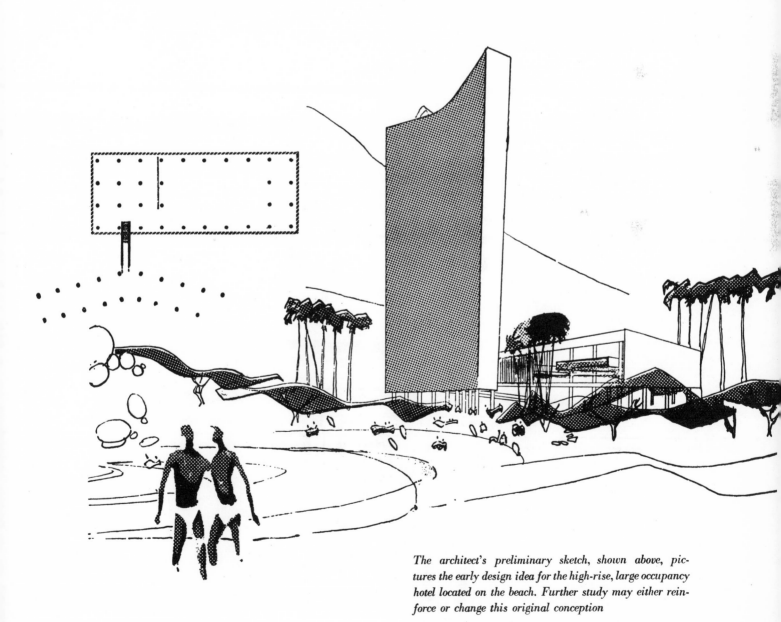

The architect's preliminary sketch, shown above, pictures the early design idea for the high-rise, large occupancy hotel located on the beach. Further study may either reinforce or change this original conception

NEIGHBORHOOD PUBLIC

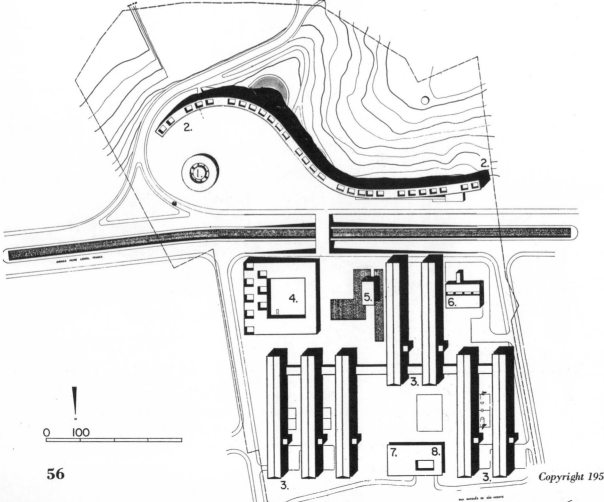

Pedregulho and Gavea
Neighborhood Housing Units

Departamento de Habitacão Popular
City of Rio de Janeiro, Brazil

Architect: Affonso Eduardo Reidy

The municipality of Rio de Janeiro—to forestall slum growth and provide housing for its small wage earners—initiated a program of "neighborhood housing units" in various parts of the city, for which architect Reidy drew experimental plans. The first to be constructed was Pedregulho; the next was Gavea; others will follow. The results to date are admirable—as civic improvements and as architectural achievements.

Carlos Botelho (above), Foto Jerry (below)

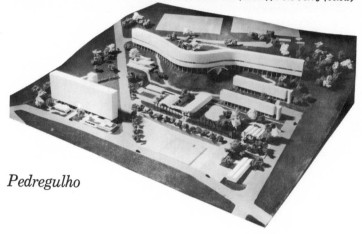

Pedregulho

HOUSING UNITS IN RIO DE JANEIRO

The thinking back of the programming and development of public housing in Rio is nicely explained by architect Affonso Reidy, who says, "It is slowly beginning to be understood by the public—and more importantly by authorities—that the problem of providing public housing has altered radically. Just as all our lives have changed and become more complex, so also have the services and amenities required by modern living. In addition to the basic, normal needs such as space, light, power, etc., there must now be—as well—planned medical and pediatric centers, school units, religious and social centers, several kinds of recreation areas, etc. In fact, the plan must include all those facilities which create a neighborhood capable of providing a full and satisfying life for its residents.

"The lack of such amenities, or their mis-planning, along with

Gavea

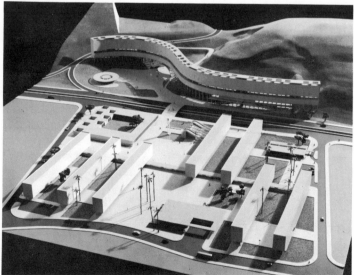

Marcel Gautherot

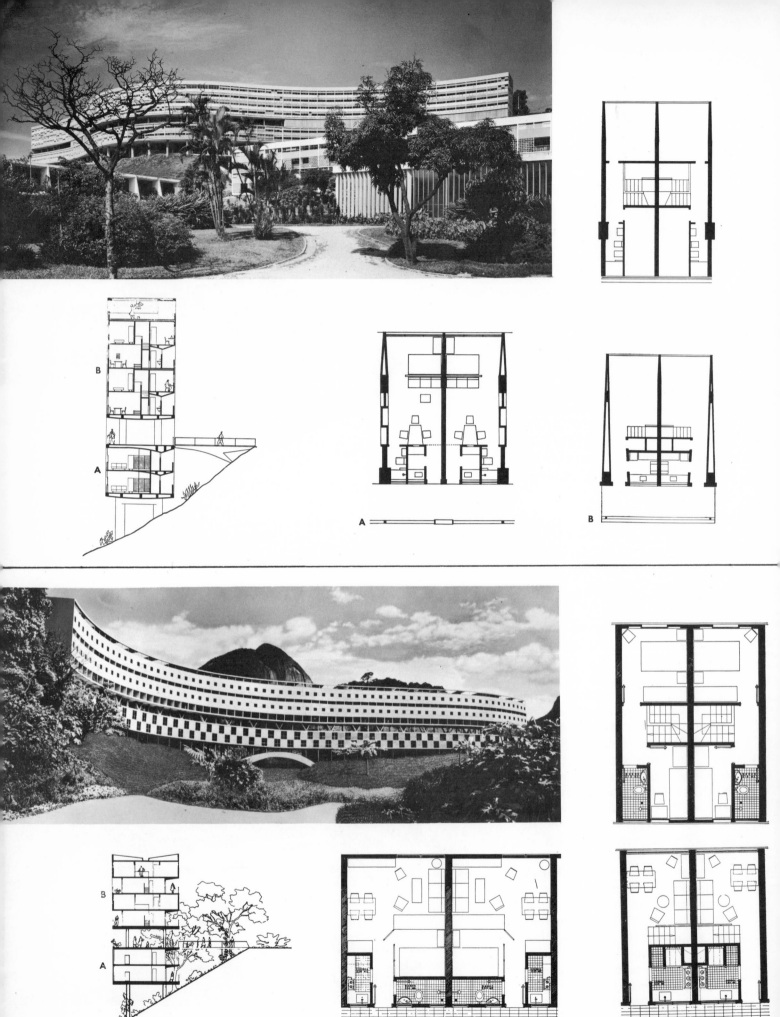

58   HOUSING UNITS IN RIO DE JANEIRO

the absence of an organized social welfare service, are the major causes of the occurrence of slums and the various social ills that we associate with slum areas."

Pedregulho and Gavea are both built on sharply sloping sites against hillsides, with the large upper apartment building curved to follow the contour of the hill. In these buildings (called Type I for the plans at left) the top 4 floors are duplex units (B), the lower 2 floors are one-room units (A), and the intermediate, mostly open level is devoted to sheltered play area such as covered access and circulation, s... ... social welfare, r...

In both proj... ...plete separation... motor traffic s... culation to all ... gram for each ...

was establishe... sus of future r... housing depar... houses 570 f... demographic ... per 100 sq yd... dates 750 fam... sity of 3 pers...

Each plan ... adult and chil... primary scho... health center,... ten, and nurs... tion, Gavea h... ter, while Ped... ming pool, g... dren's cantee...

On the foll... apartment pl... buildings (T... Note that w... mally 3-bedr... apartments c... of the bedroo... 2- and 4-be... Such flexibili... ful in admini...

Pedregulho, Type I

All photos these 2 pages: Aertsens Michel

Apartments and Dormitories

Despite the steady growth of multiple dwelling construction in the past ten years, very little has been published on this important building type. Persistent requests for more information have resulted in the editors of *Architectural Record* selecting some 53 projects for analysis in this new book.

Here are superior examples of recent multiple dwelling architecture, arranged in four groups: community-scale projects, large projects, small projects, and campus dormitories and apartments. Many noted architects are represented here, including Frank Lloyd Wright, Mies van der Rohe, Edward Stone, Marcel Breuer and Richard Neutra.

Excellent photographs, sketches and plans do much to make each project more meaningful; in all, there are over 450 illustrations. In addition to the 53 projects, the first section, *Building Multiple Dwellings*, includes discussions of housing patterns, housing expenditures, social problems of apartment design, cutting construction costs, and other pertinent material.

APARTMENTS AND DORMITORIES is of obvious value to architects, designers, engineers, contractors, real estate developers and managers, and housing authorities at all governmental levels.

Gavea, Type I

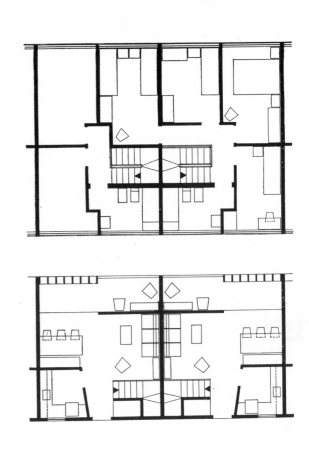

Marcel Gautherot

Pedregulho, Type II

Gavea, Type II

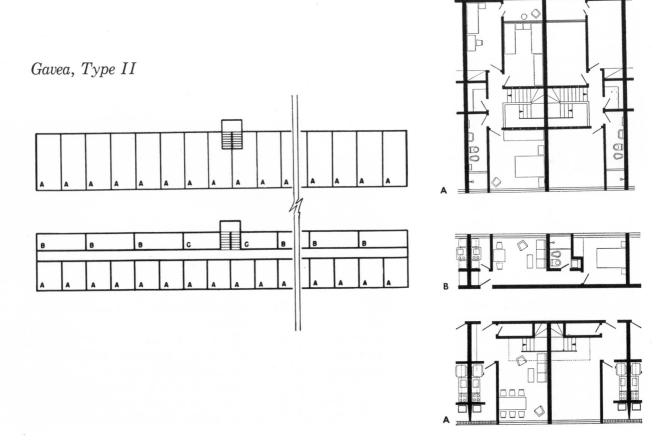

PARK FOREST, ILLINOIS

PROVING GROUND FOR COMMUNITY PLANNING TECHNIQUES

American Community Builders, Inc., Philip M. Klutznick, President

Loebl, Schlossman & Bennett, Architects and Planners

Elbert Peets, Consultant, Site and Town Planning

Kincaid & Hutchinson, City Planners and Architects (Planners, Sub-division Area)

Consoer, Townsend & Associates, Consulting Engineers

Hedrich-Blessing Studio Photo

1 *(see plan page 65)*

PARK FOREST is a new town, not a housing project. This distinction gives it significance, as a proving ground for a wide variety of planning theories. As such it becomes, fortunately but inadvertently, a test area for the sort of ideas that architects and planners will be called upon to produce in developing new communities for mobilization industries. It is especially noteworthy in showing the extent to which planning must take account of social and political problems of a community which must pull itself up by its boot straps.

In the five years since its conception, Park Forest has encountered virtually every theory, every problem, of community planning and building. It has made its own way — it is strictly private enterprise — without any governmental munificence; indeed red tape is not the least of its troubles. It has had to improvise on many an unanticipated problem — such as how to get a cemetery started, or how to decide the dogs-vs.-no-dogs question. In short it has experienced all of the thrills and pangs of bringing forth a new American town via the method of scientific planning.

The decision to tackle it this way was quite deliberate. Park Forest is an attempt to prove that the planning method can produce better communities than the Topsy

For other planners, the reasons Park Forest did not develop along different lines are probably as interesting as the reasons for its present form.

The Neighborhood Concept. — The earliest sketches show well defined areas centered about elementary schools with greenbelt carefully separating one from another. This schematic approach was abandoned for a number of reasons:

1. Because it came to be felt that communities of people exist only because of common interests, and for most interests

approach. It is an attempt, moreover, to do it all by the most enlightened social concepts, to prove that this is good business.

As a matter of fact, Park Forest has represented some fairly enlightened searches for new ways to make a dollar, or a nickel, out of the great "game" of subdividing and building. Philip M. Klutznick, its president and personal powerhouse, says that Park Forest tries to go the meat-packing industry one better, and utilize the squeal as well as the ham.

In evaluating Park Forest, it is important to remember the difference between creating a town and building a housing project. This distinction was clearly established early in the project, and it affected a great many important decisions. A housing project, for example, would not have ventured so far from Chicago (28 miles), and would not have tackled so many problems of site development, provision of utilities, schools, churches, shops, or the tricky problems of establishing new governmental units, new school boards, police and fire departments, and so on. Chicago provides an economic base for Park Forest, but the new town had to be far enough removed to be able to establish its own patterns.

Business Principles

The objective of creating a town was by no means altruistic or idealistic in purpose. It was for profit. The basic premise was that a subdivider or builder creates many values on which he does not realize. He takes his quick profit on the main items, land and buildings, but neglects the buying power newly concentrated in the community. American Community Builders envisioned a larger operation, with a substantial number of rental units under long-term ownership, a profitable shopping center, several sidelines, on the theory that this was the way to profitable operation without excessive income from one single item, such as rents.

In the beginning the progenitors foresaw the possibility of building and reselling electric power (submetering), reselling gas, selling their own water, oper-

adults will have to go outside the elementary school perimeter for major recreation, their particular church, their particular club, for interests such as dramatics, fire department, stamp club, and so on.

2. Even the school district must have flexible boundaries as school population changes in number and age group in each area.

3. Another factor to remember is that for the same length of utilities one has the choice of open space between buildings or between groups of buildings.

4. Too close identification with a small part of the total town can prevent the best attitude toward the total town — as it is, there is very strong attachment of those in each parking court, so much so that studies by students of government have pointed out the factionalism that exists in the growing political structure.

The railway lines at the north for a long time suggested an extension of commuter service and location of the shopping center at that point. It slowly became apparent that, due to costly engineering, a station would be far in the future, and bus transportation would be prime, and a central location for shopping was indicated.

The southern half of the site is relatively hilly for Chicago; the central area was a golf course so that the fairways and trees became the basis of some planning. It is interesting to note that on steep areas adjusting buildings to contours is self-evident, but on almost flat areas it can be sensitively done to minimize drainage problems again arriving at a relatively "free" plan.

ating their own bus lines, and so on, in addition to owning and leasing rental units and store buildings, not to mention all of those items repeated in an industrial subdivision on adjoining land.

Business Results

These sidelines have not all developed, but the main items are proving out well. The sub-metering idea largely disappeared in the practical matter of getting

shoppers from a substantial surrounding area, as new stores are added and as people come to appreciate the convenience, the pleasantness and the parking space of the center.

Lesson No. 1

The many complications of so sweeping a beginning as Park Forest produced the first lesson in community building. In Klutznick's words it is "that no organiza-

2   (see plan opposite page)

3

into operation a really large installation of utilities, though the company does operate its own water system on a commercial basis. The bus lines similarly went to an existing outside enterprise.

The shopping center seemed to loom larger, however, as the project developed. The shops are leased to merchandising companies on a selective basis, and company income will grow as store volume increases and as new shops add to the center.

Shopping center tenants have a solid base of purchasing power in 3000 families already in the rental units. And the house-for-sale program, now just really started, will add another 3000 to 5000 families directly located in Park Forest. Studies have shown, moreover, that the shopping center may be expected to attract

tion has all of the skills necessary to do the complete job. . . . It is wise to proceed from the premise that wherever an activity or skill is available through another organization, that organization should be utilized. . . . We in Park Forest could well have gone into the bus business. There were some who cast up figures showing that starting from an initial loss we could build into a nice profit. . . . In spite of this we sought out an existing bus transportation company, utilized their skills and absorbed portions of their early losses, rather than to go into the business ourselves." Much the same thing happened in gas service, and in electric service. Even though Park Forest anticipated its problems of utilities, it had occasion again and again to be impressed with the magnitude of the task, and its importance.

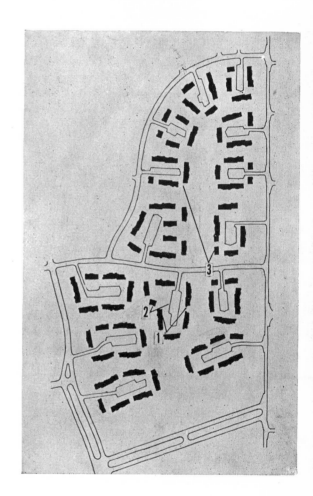

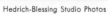

Hedrich-Blessing Studio Photos

Basis of residential planning in the rental area is a scheme of courts and malls. Buildings are grouped around a parking court (there are no garages), but the space between groups of buildings is kept open to form a fairly continuous mall. The courts tend to become informal and active — each has a small "tot yard." The more open areas appear more formal and are quieter. The parking courts identify a neighborhood group and tie close neighbors together through daily activity. The open areas tend to tie groups of buildings together and broaden the outlook somewhat

Utilities for Mobilization Housing

Turning to the problems of other new communities, Klutznick says: "From purely a physical point of view, my experience in the last war [administrator, Federal Public Housing Authority] and the experience in Park Forest lead me to believe that the basic problem that will confront community development is the lack of adequate utility installations in the areas of need. The growth of our population and the deferral, over many years through the depression and the last war, of utility replacement programs as well as extension programs, will find us in a difficult position, if the mobilization authorities embark on any degree of dispersal into new areas without simultaneously considering the demands of the population that will have to man the machinery. I see nothing in the current scene to make me happy in the thought that we learned our lesson. The building of houses is the easiest part of the mobilization housing job. The big problem, from a physical point of view, is to develop the first plan, provide adequate sewage disposal, water and other essential utilities without which a house becomes merely an outhouse. These problems we had to face in Park Forest and we believe we conquered them.

"The three ingredients in the handling of the physical problems are a good and feasible plan, ingenuity in its execution and available funds, either one's own or through a public body. Long ago, I took the position that in any future mobilization program, the first and most important step is to ascertain quite early the areas that will be affected by expansion and to undertake to extend or create the necessary basic utility systems. Without such steps, tremendous waste of time, men, money and material is inevitable."

Social Aspects of Community Building

"The principle that has been enunciated above (use outside skills), which had motivated us on the fronts indicated, has also been a guide in our treatment of community problems, such as municipal government, fire and police protection, medical care, schools and churches. We have been, and still continue to be, criticized for our position.

"There are some people who feel that we should do many things ourselves which we agree could be done more quickly and perhaps at less cost, but with ultimate disadvantage to the growth of the community. We have taken the position that public authorities, school officials, the people themselves, whether they be tenant or home owner, must be involved in the community building process from the beginning and must assume their share of the load in terms of administration, thinking and execution. We have never side-stepped our contributory responsibilities in terms of dollars.

"For example, on the church front, before a single line was drawn in our plan for Park Forest, the Church Federation of Metropolitan Chicago, the Cardinal's office, the Lutheran Synod, which is not in the Federa-

Loebl, Schlossman & Bennett planned the shopping center to be informal in layout, efficient in merchandising methods, and gay and attractive in appearance. The plan seems quite free and casual, but actually it is carefully worked out for good merchandising. It has no focal point, no "100 per cent location," no obvious concentration of traffic, since the parking space virtually surrounds it. Free forms of the store buildings bothered the tenants in the negotiation stage, but they soon learned that the buildings

were thoughtfully planned for selling, even though they didn't meet standard layouts of chain stores, and came to appreciate that the free forms sprang from the true selling function. Store buildings are kept in a uniform white, and store tenants have been glad to sacrifice their traditional colored fronts for the pleasant brightness of the center. The shopping center is lighted at night, as a bright center of attraction. Covered walks shelter pedestrians between stores — no auto traffic can enter the center itself, though there are access turn-arounds at several points so that cars can come close for heavy packages. Landscaping will add a note of gaiety, and contribute to a fair-like spirit that is an especial objective of the planners tion, and the Episcopal Bishop, who likewise is not in the Federation, were involved in the planning aspects. We agreed to and have contributed improved land; but we have insisted, as a condition to that contribution, that they organize their congregations and assume the responsibility for structures. There have been some delays. You don't build a solid church structure on prayer without action, even if that sounds blasphemous. Consequently, we have only one church completed, the Trinity Lutheran Church. The Catholic school, church and accessory buildings are well along and should be completed within a few months. The United Protestant Church is out for bids next week, as is the Episcopal Church. Ministers and a priest were long ago stationed in Park Forest and they and their adherents are building the churches.

"In connection with the school problem, which in many ways has been the most aggravating of them all, particularly under the Illinois law, we have pursued a similar course. The largest part of our development lies in what was once a rural district which never had enough resources to support even a minimum schoolhouse for its 20 pupils. That portion of Park Forest lying in this district was withdrawn and the school district of our own tenants was established at the beginning. From the start, we outlined a program in our own thinking which from time to time we negotiated with the school board. In view of tax lag and bonding power lag, we undertook to subsidize the school board by contributing to their budget for the last two years. We provided temporary facilities during that same period of time. Together we established a non-profit corporation to build the first permanent schools, to which our company contributed the necessary funds. The first permanent school building is in the process of completion. When it is complete and as soon as the school board has the necessary bonding power in a few months after its completion, under their contract with us they will acquire it and issue the bonds. The second school goes out for bids this month and will be built on exactly the same pattern. A third school is scheduled to start before the end of the year. By this process, it is true that we have involved our company financially, but what to me is more important, the people themselves have had their feet thoroughly wetted in the problems of school administration, school budgets, school operation, so that we can properly look forward to one of the best school systems in this whole area, when it has matured in the next few years.

"In general public administration, we have pursued a similar course. We encouraged the incorporation of the village when we only had 150 families resident in Park Forest. We were operating a private police force and using a contract service for fire protection. In the first year we contributed to the new village sufficient funds so that they could get the Department of Public Safety organized. We have a crackajack police department, small but effective, and a top-notch volunteer fire

Hedrich-Blessing Studio Photos

Jewel Tea was the first of the larger store tenants in Park Forest. The building done for their tenancy by Loebl, Schlossman & Bennett was something of a surprise to the chain's merchandising experts, but has proved to be fine for selling. Aisles for grocery items run diagonally, pointing toward checking counters. By the simple device of tilting the large trusses the architects have given the store a clerestory; the sloping ceiling adds noticeably to the openness which a clerestory section seems always to contribute

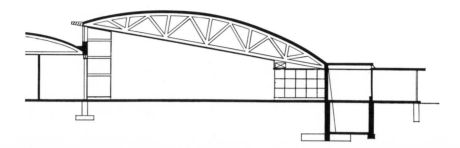

TYPICAL THREE-AND-A-HALF ROOM UNIT, IN "TWIN HOUSE" BUILDING

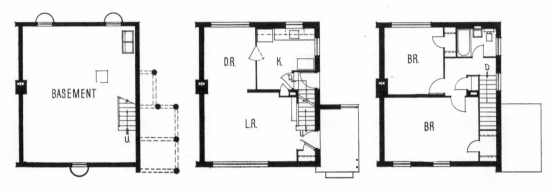

TYPICAL FIVE-ROOM UNIT, TWIN-HOUSE TYPE

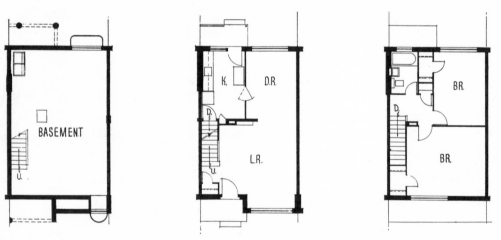

TYPICAL FIVE-ROOM UNIT, ROW-HOUSE TYPE

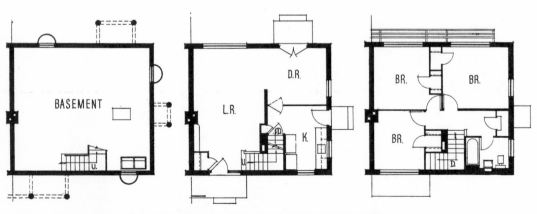

TYPICAL SIX-ROOM UNIT, TWIN-HOUSE TYPE

3   9   15 18 FT

department to whom we contributed the first two pieces of equipment. It would not be fair to say that all these things happened easily. Quite to the contrary, there were periods when it would have been much easier for us to discharge functions ourselves than to haggle and argue with people who were learning the practical aspects of building a town. But as a result, we have a maturing town government with a sense of responsibility growing each day. We have a public plan commission and a town hall that is in process of erection.

"On the medical care and public health front, we have not made as much patent progress. We do have a citizens' public health committee. We have interested

of criticism, I must point out that it probably could not have been otherwise. Government is subject to pressures to a greater degree than we are as a private company. Not only is it subject to pressures, but it does not have the same type of balance sheet with which to compare itself as we do. While we believe that we are a thoroughly enlightened type of company in this field, nevertheless, we are inhibited by practical considerations from yielding to the point of committing business suicide. Our income and outgo must at least balance in our determining how far we may want to go in meeting the demands of residents in Park Forest. This is a strong barrier against outright disproportions.

Hedrich-Blessing Studio Photos

a group of doctors and public health specialists who are planning for the day when the hospital and medical center will emerge; the latter, not too far off, the former some way off. We are just beginning to formalize steps on a community recreational program. Here again the principal stimulus comes from the people and what we ultimately develop here will be that which they want and, we hope, can afford.

"By example, I have tried to illustrate our basic philosophy. One of the great failures in government operation of villages and towns that it was compelled to build or undertook as an experiment was the great difficulty it had in withdrawing from responsibilities that it once assumed. Another inequity, perhaps, was the development of public services of a gilded character and altogether beyond the capacity of the people who live in the town to pay for. In connection with this type

"Probably more important than dollar consideration is the fact that the method that we have pursued, in my opinion, tends to fill more people with a sense of responsibility and certainly makes them more knowledgeable, in the fields of public concern. As one public official who visited Park Forest once said, 'This is probably the most significant school in civics in all of our country'. Our population is primarily youthful. They are people who would be lost in the jungles of great metropolitan communities. Perhaps they would live their entire lives in such a community without knowing the significance of a school budget, what it takes to make a fire department or police department run, or how you pay for any of the things that are implicit in public operation. Many of these people are bright and able people with fine academic background who, if they continued to live in large metropolitan centers, probably never would become members of plan commissions, school boards, village boards, recreational committees or public health committees. Here in the impressionable stage of their lives they have been compelled to assume significant responsibilities in their community. It would be foolhardy to say that all have met the challenge. But it would be untrue not to state that the growth and understanding of many has been something at which to marvel.

"What has all this to do with the potential contribution of what we term private enterprise in the forthcoming mobilization effort? Nothing more than to point out that the government would be well advised to lay the ground work to perform only those tasks which it must essentially perform in order to keep the mobilization machinery going. In the field of town development in areas completely rural and desolate in character, government must substitute for non-existing public agencies on an interim basis to finance utilities, schools and similar public services. Beyond that, to the extent that the people to be served can afford the production, private enterprise should be called upon to do the job. There can be a melding of responsibilities which should result in the development of permanent communities in which the government does not stay as a vested interest exposed to all of the pressures and responsibilities which it is not established to discharge. By collaborative interest we can build communities in which the people who live there discharge the normal functions of communities."

Planning Park Forest

While details of the original scheme have changed, the basic concept and its major elements have remained

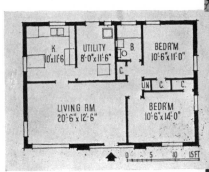

constant, and Park Forest has developed according to its schedule. There was one major change — the rental units were built first instead of houses for sale. One reason was the great need in postwar years for rental units, especially for married veterans. Also 608 financing made rental units particularly attractive. The main reason, though, was that building rental units was the

Just getting under way is the house-for-sale program at Park Forest. Houses are built directly by American Community Builders. One floor plan is repeated many times, with variations in exterior detailing. Carl J. Kastrup was architect for most units

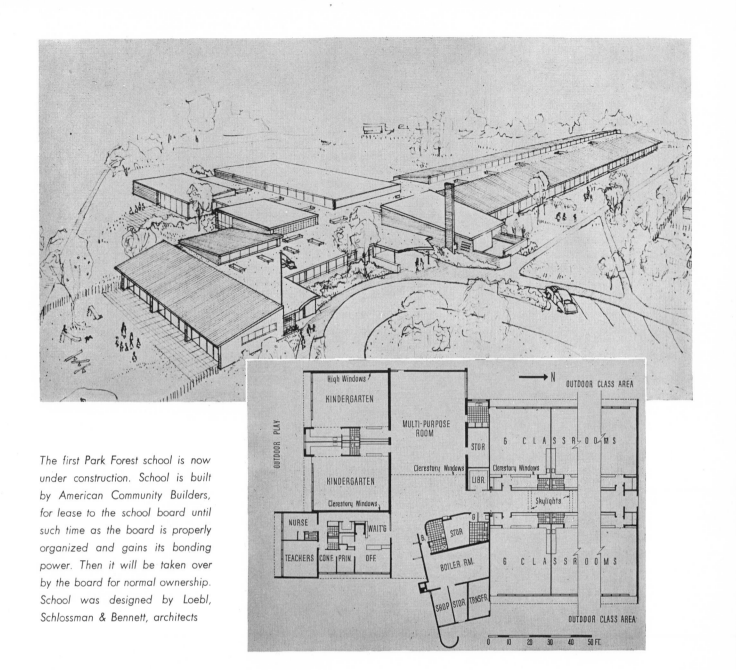

The first Park Forest school is now under construction. School is built by American Community Builders, for lease to the school board until such time as the board is properly organized and gains its bonding power. Then it will be taken over by the board for normal ownership. School was designed by Loebl, Schlossman & Bennett, architects

Hedrich-Blessing Studio Photos

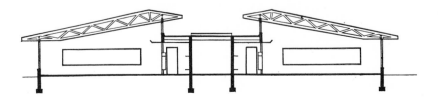

quickest way to get Park Forest into being and give it identity. Three thousand families, coming in quickly, would permit a sizeable start on the shopping center, would bring quick income to get schools, churches and so on started. Only now are the houses for sale really in volume production.

There was some careful figuring in the determination of the figure of 3000 rental units. This number seemed to assert itself strongly, coming largely from the requirements for utilities — the initial installation was of necessity so large that no lesser number of units would be feasible.

Then it was necessary to do some selling to arrange financing for so large a group. Once the initial shock was absorbed, however, there was no difficulty, and the FHA granted approval on nine separate mortgages totalling $27,600,000, the largest single commitment made. Three life insurance companies share in the mortgages — New York Life, Sun Life of Canada, and Northwestern Mutual.

The principal here is important — starting a new community is a big undertaking, with a huge investment in land acquisition, planning, roadways, utilities, etc., and these investments fix a certain minimum number of units to assure sound operation. Park Forest might have got along with 2000 at first, but 3000 was a much better figure. And the necessary speed was much easier with rental units than with houses for sale. There were real difficulties at the start nevertheless — for a while the symbol of Park Forest was MUD, and the operation was almost mired in complaints — but the tenants came as fast as buildings could be completed, and Park Forest was successfully launched.

Prefabs in Park Forest

Park Forest has been probably the largest potential customer for prefabricated houses, although almost none have been built there. With all of the building troubles after the war, there was much enthusiasm for prefabs. It seemed quite logical, for prefabs might help get many families in quickly, solve construction difficulties, save time, and help in that perennial problem of the lag between investment and recovery of funds.

At one time Park Forest placed an order for 2000 Lustron houses, but none were ever delivered, for Lustron's difficulties caught up with them just at that time. Virtually every other prefab offering has been carefully investigated, and a few houses are included in the test group now. But no large contract was actually placed.

Most potential deals failed over a basic point. American Community Builders knew they would have to do heavy selling and promotion to win buyers' acceptance, especially in a large, quick operation. They asked for sales help from the prefab companies, in the form of discounts to permit necessary advertising. But no house

Hedrich-Blessing Studio Photos

Trinity Lutheran Church was the first built in Park Forest; Loebl, Schlossman & Bennett, architects. It is really the chapel section of the full project, to be completed when the congregation grows

Design for the United Church, Park Forest;
Schweikher and Elting, architects

maker could then agree to grant this "trade discount," even for the mass selling operation that was involved. So Park Forest is building its own houses.

Houses for Sale

The houses-for-sale program finally did not get into actual construction until last fall, when work began on 525 two-bedroom "ranch" houses, with masonry walls and radiant heat. The first 100 were completed about April 1, 1951.

The next 300 houses, it is expected, may still be pre-fabs, with three bedrooms. Then will follow 800 more, conventional or prefab depending on public acceptance and demand. For next year it is contemplated to go into different types and sizes of houses, although Park Forest will probably remain a small-house development.

It is a source of considerable satisfaction to Mr. Klutznick that of the first 100 houses sold, 35 went to tenants in Park Forest. And, he adds with a grin, they are already forming a home-owners' association. "Maybe now there will be somebody organizing to save taxes instead of spend them."

Proposed synagogue for Park Forest; Loebl, Schlossman & Bennett, architects and engineers

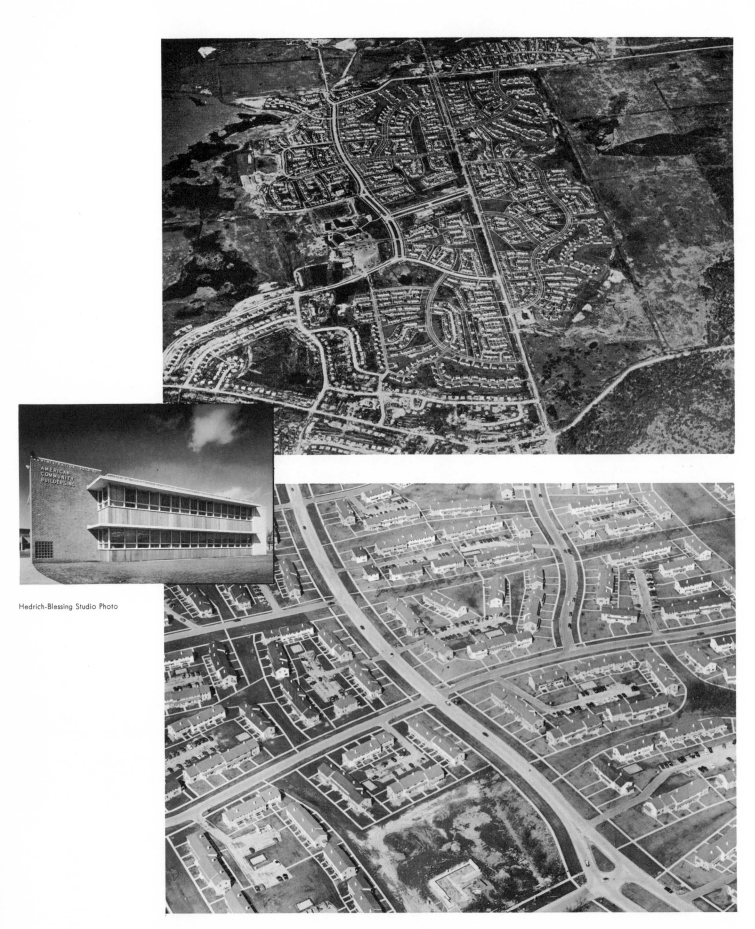

Hedrich-Blessing Studio Photo

Harry Williams Aerial Photos

III

Apartments: Large Projects

APARTMENT HOUSES

Prepared by John Hancock Callender, A.I.A.

A VAST AMOUNT OF PLANNING INGENUITY has gone into the development of the typical middle-class elevator apartment. The starting point has always been the high cost of elevators, the goal to make the elevators serve as many apartments as possible.

The typical plan that has emerged is in the shape of a cross with the elevators at the center. Corridors down the center of each wing give access to apartments on each side. Site conditions or the size of the lot may require one or more of the wings to be shortened or even eliminated. The resulting T-shaped plan is frequently seen; the Lee Apartments in Salem, Oregon (page 83) is a good example. Where land values are higher a tower version of the cross plan is often used. In this scheme public corridors are eliminated and the two apartments in each wing open directly off the elevator lobby. The Cornell Arms in Columbia, South Carolina (page 82) is of this type. As indicated by these two examples, one from the southeast, the other from the northwest, there is nothing regional about the typical apartment building. Examples can be found in practically every city.

The defects of the cross plan are the long corridors, whether public or private, the use of the living room as a corridor and poor internal circulation in general, lack of cross-ventilation, and complete disregard of orientation whether for sun, breeze or view. The living room, which should be the pleasantest room in the apartment, tends to be buried in the reentrant angle of the building, its small window embarrassingly close to the neighbor's window.

A recent improvement on the tower type is shown in the Army Twin Towers in Chicago (page 84) with its square plan. Better livability has been achieved at the cost of fewer apartments per elevator. In the exciting design for River Ledge at Hastings-on-Hudson, N. Y. (page 85) the basic rule of elevator economy has been discarded. With only two apartments per elevator, every defect of the cross plan has been eliminated.

Although influences in architecture usually move down the social and economic scale, one important influence in apartment design has come from below. The typical plan developed for public housing was the two- or three-story walk-up with two apartments per stair per floor. People soon became uncomfortably aware that these low-rent apartments provided a degree of cross-ventilation, privacy, and orientation that were unobtainable at any price in the typical elevator apartment. River Ledge is nothing more than this scheme plus elevators and other amenities.

Other attempts to combine the advantages of the walk-up apartment and the elevator building have been along two general lines. One device that has been more often used abroad than here is the exterior corridor. In this scheme all apartments have through ventilation, with some loss of privacy. The Cooperative Residences in Chicago (page 88) and the Angamos Apartments in Lima, Peru (page 89) are of this type, although both are walk-ups. The other approach is the one described by Mr. Funaro (page 21) resulting in the scheme known as "skip-floor" or "skip-stop," where the elevators stop only at every third or fourth floor. Apartments on the intervening floors can have through ventilation and full privacy at the price of walking up one floor or down two. The west building at 100 East Erie (page 87) is an example of this scheme. There is no reason in theory why these two methods could not be combined with the result that an exterior corridor would occur only at every third or fourth floor.

Air conditioning may give the typical cross plan a new lease on life. Natural ventilation and orientation cease to be factors in an air conditioned apartment, and small sealed windows would reduce the lack of privacy. The day may even come when interior rooms are acceptable and this could have a profound effect on apartment house planning. If each unit were to have only one of its four or five rooms on an outside wall, apartment houses might assume the massive shapes generally associated with loft buildings.

The very small apartment house, less than ten families say, is an entirely different building type. Small scale, non-fireproof materials, and an intimate relation to site and landscaping, make the small apartment closely akin to the single family house. As might be expected, many of these small apartments, such as the one shown on page 164, have been designed by architects who are known for their work in the small house field. Another example of this type of building comes from Mississippi (page 167).

All housing today suffers from insufficient space, and apartments are even more cramped than houses. This fact comes into sharpest focus in kitchens. Does preparing a meal take any less space in an apartment than in a house? Yet in many apartments which are otherwise well designed, the kitchens are much smaller than in houses of comparable size, and are completely inadequate when judged by the standards developed by the Small Homes Council of the University of Illinois.

Another defect of most apartments is their disregard of the powerful human desire for some outdoor living space and a chance to grow a few things. Balconies or porches should be standard items in apartment house design — not decorative balconies, but usable ones — not for a few tenants, but for all. That balconies need not be limited to warm countries is shown by recent experience in Cambridge, Mass., and long experience in Sweden.

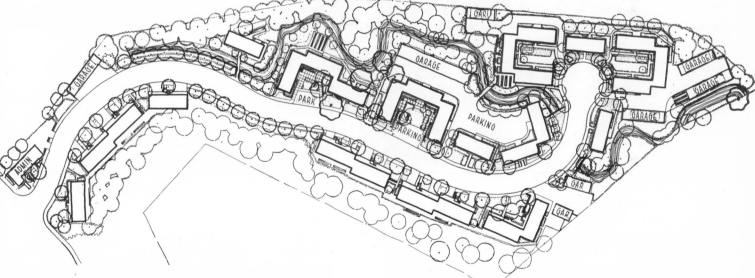

CASTLEMONT GARDENS, OAKLAND, CALIFORNIA

John Carl Warnecke, Architect

THE DEVELOPMENT of a successful 608* project on this all but impossible site was a considerable triumph for both architect and owner. The irregular tract consisted of the steep-sided and heavily wooded valley of a meandering creek. Containing no buildable land by conventional standards, the valley had been by-passed by the rapidly expanding city. The site was further handicapped by the existence of a trunk sewer

with three branches, each with a 10- or 15-ft easement, which cut into the valley.

As though the physical difficulties of the site were not enough, the developers were also faced with a legal obstacle; the entire tract was zoned for single-family houses. Even though the property was completely isolated from the surrounding community by steep and for the most part heavily wooded slopes, with access possible only at the westerly end which was already zoned for commercial use, several hundred neighboring property owners fought long and vigorously against the requested rezoning.

A 608 project is a multi-family dwelling built under the provisions of Title 608 of the National Housing Act. This legislation specified that FHA would guarantee 90 per cent of the mortgage of multi-family projects if the site and building conformed to FHA standards. Title 608 was discontinued several years ago.

Typical unit plan (below) shows the larger than average rooms and the two stairways which serve each unit. Main stair is well protected from the weather

The total development consists of 140 two-bedroom apartments in 15 two- and three-story buildings. Although the project had to be designed for operation as a single unit, it was necessary in order to obtain the most favorable financing under FHA to divide it into eight separate projects, each costing less than $200,000. Each division was required to conform to all FHA and city regulations and to be complete within itself, including garages, utilities, laundry rooms, and storage lockers.

The basic plan is a two-bedroom apartment with a gross area of almost 1000 sq ft. The result is rooms which are considerably less cramped than in the average 608 apartment. Although there are only two apartments per floor, there is a main and a service stair serving each apartment. Both are technically exterior stairs but the main stair is well protected from the weather, being almost entirely within the building line. The balcony-like stair landings have been made a feature of the exterior design and serve to give the project its principal architectural interest.

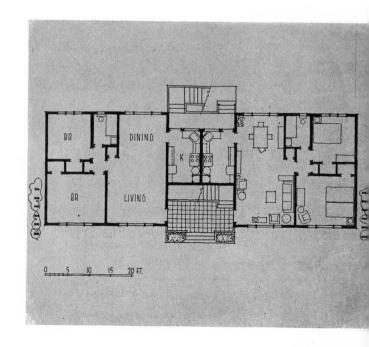

Rondal Partridge Photos

Below: service court and garages. Below, right: the stream which winds through the length of the property had to be repeatedly bridged and culverted

CORNELL ARMS, COLUMBIA, SOUTH CAROLINA

Stork & Lyles, Architects; Bissett, Carlisle & Wolff, Associates

THE COMPACT SERVICE CORE contains two elevators, a pair of scissor stairs, incinerator and air conditioning equipment. Public corridors are almost eliminated and entrance corridors are not over 10 ft in length. Each of the three typical wings contains two two-bedroom apartments. The shorter wing contains one three-bedroom and two-bath unit; this apartment is so arranged that one bedroom and bath can be rented separately. All baths are interior, even when located on outside walls. Unusual in a building of this type is that each apartment has its own storage room. Windows are small, since the building is air conditioned.

Sigurd Fischer

TYPICAL FLOOR

LEE APARTMENTS, SALEM, OREGON

Victor N. Jones & Associates, Architects and Engineers

THIS 101-FAMILY APARTMENT HOUSE is located on a corner lot facing on a park mall leading to the capitol two blocks away. The business district is about the same distance. There are 39 efficiency apartments, 50 one-bedroom and 12 two-bedroom units in the seven-story building. Average room count is 2.73. Average rents are $31.73 per room or $86.86 per unit per month. Construction is reinforced concrete painted on exterior.

Service core contains one elevator with provision for a second and one stair. At end of each wing is another stair or a fire escape. Parking space is provided under the rear wing of the building.

Jim Morris

TYPICAL FLOOR

Hedrich-Blessing

ARMY TWIN TOWERS APARTMENTS, CHICAGO

A. Epstein and Sons, Architects and Engineers

THIS 252-UNIT DEVELOPMENT was constructed under Title VIII of the FHA for the housing of military personnel and civilian employees of the Fifth Army. The two identical buildings are approximately square in plan and 22 stories high. The service core consists of two elevators and a scissor stair with the public corridor wrapped around three sides. This scheme permits better unit plans than in most elevator apartments. Interior baths and kitchens permit all exterior walls to be devoted to major rooms. These rooms are fairly shallow and since the windows extend in most cases from wall to wall, the natural lighting is exceptionally good.

Construction is of reinforced concrete, placed by the pumpcrete method and speeding in its curing by the vacuum process for the removal of excess water. Exterior finish is brick on two sides, and stainless steel spandrels on the other two sides where the windows are continuous. Radiant heating, with individual controls will be provided by means of copper tubing embedded in the structural slabs.

RIVER LEDGE GARDEN APARTMENTS

Hastings-on-Hudson, N. Y.

Antonin Raymond and L. L. Rado
Holsman, Holsman, Klekamp and Taylor
Associated Architects

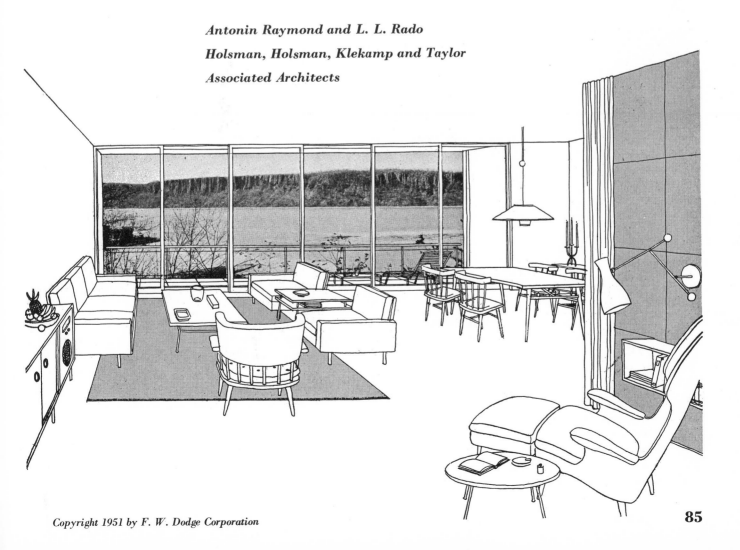

On a beautifully wooded site overlooking the Hudson River, this development has been designed to exploit a splendid view to the west. All of the 114 units in the three six-story buildings have an unobstructed view. In addition, each apartment has a balcony running the full width of the river side. Balconies are thoughtfully provided with storage space for outdoor furniture. Projecting balconies and party walls help to shield the glass wall of the apartments from the western sun. An elevator and a stair serve only two apartments per floor, with the result that all apartments have through ventilation. The sloping site permits six additional units in the basement of the center building.

Exterior wall construction is similar to that of 100 East Erie, described on the opposite page. Floor construction is hollow precast concrete slabs with radiant panel heating. Party walls are reinforced concrete. Partitions are gypsum drywall.

This project and the following one were developed under the sponsorship of the Community Development Trust of Chicago's mutual ownership plan.

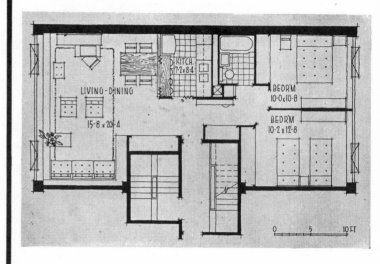

Holsman, Holsman, Klekamp and Taylor, Architects

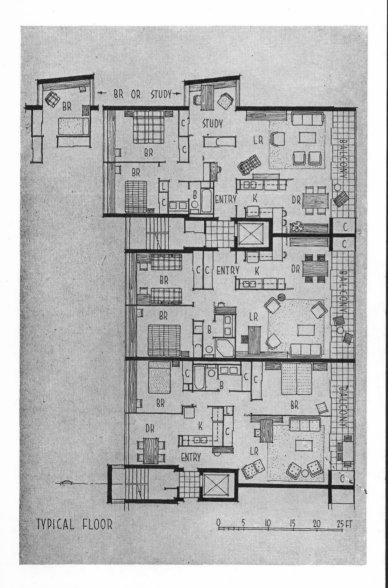

TYPICAL FLOOR

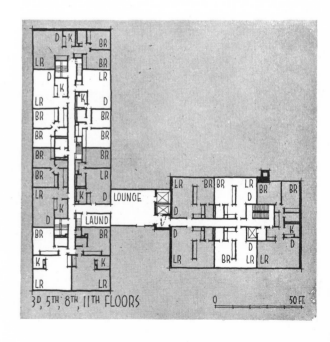

3ᴅ, 5ᵀᴴ, 8ᵀᴴ, 11ᵀᴴ FLOORS

100 EAST ERIE, CHICAGO, ILLINOIS

THIS MUTUAL OWNERSHIP DEVELOPMENT occupies the site of Cyrus McCormick's "elegant" mansion dating from the 1870's. Rising from a two-story commercial base, which features a spacious central court enlivened by planting and pool, are two apartment buildings with only the most tenuous connection. The east building contains 64 one-bedroom apartments in a conventional corridor scheme with an elevator stop at each floor. The west building utilizes the "skip-stop" scheme for its 56 two-bedroom apartments. Access to the elevators in the east building is by glass-enclosed bridge at every third floor. Service elevators in each building connect every floor with the basement, where parking for 42 cars is provided. Apartments are well planned and pleasantly open in feeling.

Wall construction is 8 in. lightweight reinforced concrete poured between exterior finish of precast brick panels, 4 by 8 ft. by 2¼ in. thick, and interior finish of precast lightweight concrete. Floors are cork tile on precast acoustical concrete slabs supported by concrete beams with permanent metal forms. Heating is radiant with individual thermostatic controls for each apartment.

CHICAGO COOPERATIVE HAS EXTERIOR CORRIDORS

Cooperative Residences, Inc., Chicago, Illinois
George Fred Keck — William Keck, Architects
Robert Bruce Tague, Associate Architect

CHICAGO FURNISHES another example of a cooperative development which avoids the routine pattern. In this small project of 23 units, an extraordinary variety of accommodation is offered. In two separate buildings there will be efficiency apartments, one and two-bedroom flats, and two and three-bedroom duplexes.

Both buildings are basementless and will be radiantly heated by means of an oil-fired hot-water system cir-culating through coils embedded in floors or ceilings. Floor construction will be precast hollow-core concrete slabs with asphalt tile finish. Windows will extend from the ceiling to within 18 in. of the floor and in many cases from wall to wall. Equipment will include storage walls and electric kitchens.

Cooperative Residences, Inc. is made up principally of professors from four nearby universities.

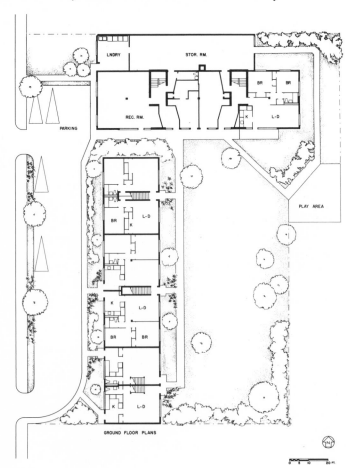

GROUND FLOOR PLANS

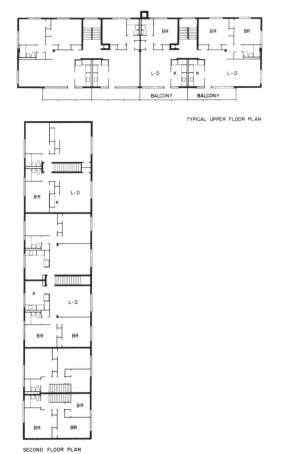

TYPICAL UPPER FLOOR PLAN

SECOND FLOOR PLAN

ANGAMOS APARTMENTS, LIMA, PERU

Santiago Agurto Calvo, Architect

IN LATIN AMERICA exterior corridors and stairs are no longer novelties. In this example from Peru the stairs are well protected from the weather and all apartments have private terraces.

In addition to 92 apartments, ranging in size from one to four bedrooms, the block-square development includes three playgrounds and a group of eight stores and a cafeteria. Off-street parking space is provided in front of the stores.

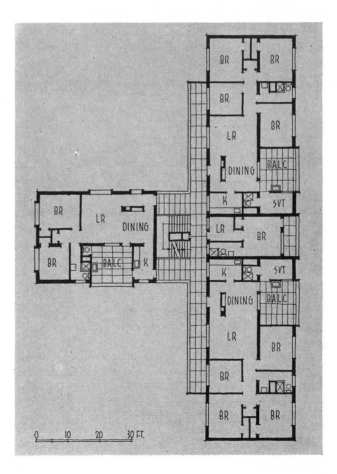

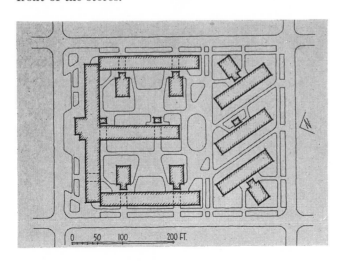

VARIETY AND OPEN SPACE FOR NEW YORK

Kips Bay Park Apartments, New York City

I. M. Pei & Associates, Architects
S. J. Kessler & Sons, Associated

Webb & Knapp, Inc., Developers

In contrast to the abandoned scheme for the same site—one which called for 7 buildings spaced over the 3-block area—this new design offers the amenity of a broad, central, landscaped plaza spreading about a reflecting pool 195 by 65 ft, with parking for 250 cars beneath.

Two 21-story apartment buildings of architectural concrete, with floor-to-ceiling glass infilling—interrupted only by 7-in.-high air conditioning units—will flank the plaza. The 410-ft-long structures will contain 1136 apartments ranging in size from studio to three-bedroom units.

A 10-story professional building for medical suites (convenient to the new hospital across the avenue) and a one-story shopping center will complete the scheme.

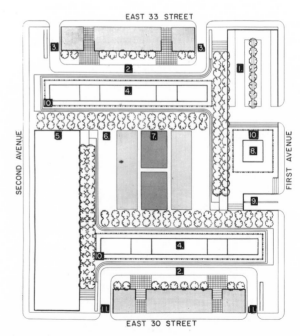

1. Parking	5. Shopping	9. Ramp Down
2. Driveway	6. Plaza	10. Arcade
3. Ramp Up	7. Reflecting Pool	11. Ramp Down
4. Apartments	8. Medical Suites	

SKIP-FLOOR ACCESS SAVES CUBAGE

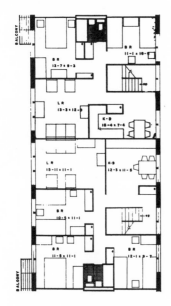 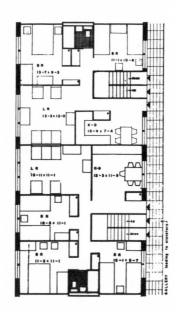 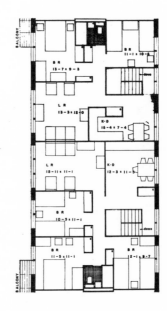

PLAN BELOW GALLERY FLOOR   PLAN OF GALLERY FLOOR   PLAN ABOVE GALLERY FLOOR

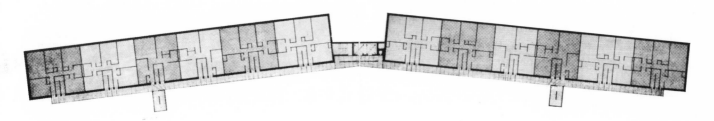

Borgia Butler Houses, Bronx, N. Y.
For The New York City Housing Authority

Joseph & Vladeck, Architects

Consultants
Landscape: Joseph Gangemi & James Rose;
Site Development: Ralph Eberlin; Structural:
Weinberger, Freiman, Leichtman & Quinn;
Mechanical: Carlson & Sweatt

Ben Schnall

These high-rise units feature a "skip-floor and gallery" arrangement in which the elevators stop only at the middle floor of every three, with further circulation laterally by gallery or vertically by a private stair of one flight. Fire stairs are placed outside, connecting the cantilevered galleries.

The architects explain that the design materially reduces space usually devoted to halls and stairs; enables all apartments (oriented east-west) to have through ventilation; reduces the cost of the $17 million project by one-quarter million.

THREE DESIGNS LEADING TO

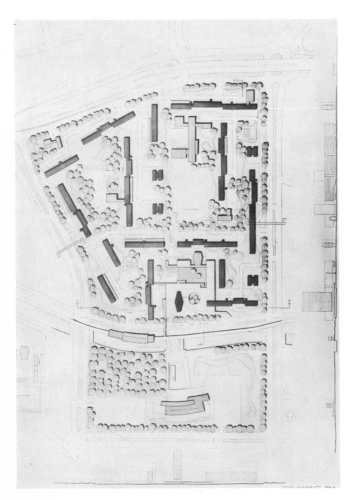

THE FINAL PLAN increases density slightly, and places particular emphasis on relating the high office block to the south with the newly finished American Library across the canal

A Neighborhood Housing Project
Mehringplatz, Berlin, Germany
For GEHAG Housing Company

The Architects Collaborative
Architects

In Charge:
Walter Gropius, Norman Fletcher

THE FIRST SCHEME disposes the buildings freely for variety of outdoor space without sacrificing in any respect sun infiltration

Architect Walter Gropius says, "This project was designed for an almost completely bombed-out area in central Berlin, around the Mehringplatz. The 53-acre site lies between the recently completed American Library and a newly designed east-west thoroughfare.

"The project demanded careful urban study of the site and the areas about it. A density of 54

A FINAL SOLUTION

families per acre was required, for a total of 2800 families. Slightly over $4000 per unit was budgeted. The following types of living units were suggested:

a. 3-bedroom units, 8-floors high; 2 units per landing.
b. 2-bedroom units, 8-floors high; open gallery access; one-family maisonettes in the first and second floors.
c. 3-bedroom units, 3-floors high; walkup type.
d. 1- & 2-bedroom units, 6 floors high; open gallery access
e. 1-bedroom units, 8 floors high; open gallery access.

"Each scheme includes the elements necessary for a complete neighborhood: primary school, churches, shops, nursery, recreation areas, and parking areas.

"Main traffic moves about the site on four sides, and the self-contained neighborhood thus encompassed is designed for unhampered pedestrian movement."

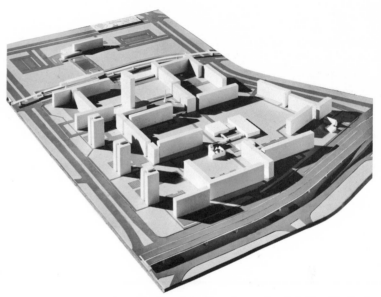

THE SECOND SCHEME interestingly relates the slab-like blocks in such a manner that a series of modified courtyards is created

THE THIRD SCHEME is more open in character. Here, the curved block is reminiscent of the round form of the old, historic Mehringplatz

NEW FACE FOR LARGE AREA IN

*The St. Louis Plaza Project
For The Urban Redevelopment Corp.
Of St. Louis*

*Hellmuth, Obata & Kassabaum
Architects & Harris Armstrong,
Architect*

*Wm. C. E. Beck er, Structural Engi-
neer; John D. Falvey, Mechanical
Engineer; Paul Tishman General
Contractor, Inc., and Fruin-Colnon
Construction Co., Joint General Con-
tractors.*

This large project—to provide
1090 apartments in six 13-story
buildings at a total cost close to
$15 million—is now under con-
struction in downtown St. Louis,
only a few blocks from the main
business section. Aimed at providing a new and more appealing

DOWNTOWN ST. LOUIS

kind of urban living for those
who *like* the city, it is designed to
lure back to urbanity those who
have deserted it for a suburban
development that so often fails
to measure up to the dream that
originally sold it.

The two existing churches on
the site will be appropriately
landscaped and will remain as an
integral part of the plan.

Balconies will add interest to
the façades, and St. Louisans—
who traditionally *use* their balconies—will find them of two
sizes and shapes, alternated to
provide an interesting exterior
pattern—with metal railings and
color.

Structural frames will be of reinforced concrete with flat slabs
—the first such in that area. Interior columns are placed to con-
form to plan divisions; a skim
coat of plaster will provide smooth
soffits that can be left as is for
painting.

Mac Mizuki

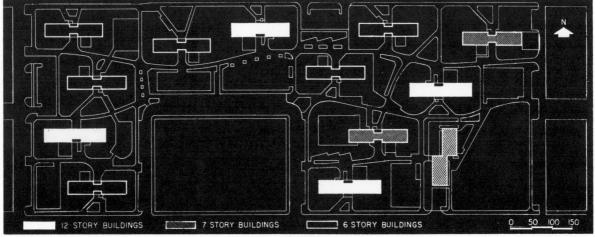

12 STORY BUILDINGS   7 STORY BUILDINGS   6 STORY BUILDINGS   0 50 100 150

Copyright 1954 by F. W. Dodge Corporation

ST. LOUIS: HIGH RISE BUILDINGS AND BALCONIES

John J. Cochran Garden Apartments for the St. Louis Housing Authority

Hellmuth, Obata & Kassabaum, Architects

John D. Falvey, Mechanical & Electrical Engineer

Wm. C. E. Becker, Structural Engineer

Horner & Shifrin, Utility Engineers

Harland Batholomew & Associates, Landscape Architects

Millstone Construction, Inc., Builders

THIS BUILDING GROUP, awarded both the Gold Medal of the St. Louis Chapter, AIA, 1953 and an Honorable Mention, Architectural League of New York, 1953 Exhibition, was designed with the primary idea of trying to achieve a residential quality combined with openness of site and to provide a maximum of social and communal facilities within the economic and planning requirements of the Public Housing Administration. The project was designed for low income families, eligibility being determined by income and number of children.

The architects say, "To achieve our goal we tried to eliminate the stigma often attached to such projects, and it was imperative to avoid a feeling of regimentation. To help accomplish this, the spaces between the buildings were as carefully studied as the units, building heights were varied, design details such as entrances were individually considered, and primary colors were used on balcony doors. This emphasis on residential quality seems to help eliminate some of the institutional aspects common to such projects and appears to justify a design approach rather than a statistical approach as a basis for planning."

The site, in a blighted area only six blocks from the central business district, was restricted in area so that openness could be achieved only by high-rise units. The land coverage is 11.3 per cent and density is 44.3 families (149 persons) per acre. In addition to outdoor recreation areas, play spaces and drying yards, the plan provides laundries, tenant storage space and storage for wheel toys at either ground floor or basement level.

An opportunity to exhibit a full size mock-up of a typical dwelling unit at a civic exposition resulted in a chance to gather the comments and criticism of the thousands who attended, and consider these in the development of the final scheme. As built, the buildings provide a maximum of privacy by means of the typical in-line plan, and are carefully oriented to catch the summer breezes important in St. Louis. Each apartment above ground level has an individual balcony to serve as a private "front porch."

Mac Mizuki

Mac Mizuki

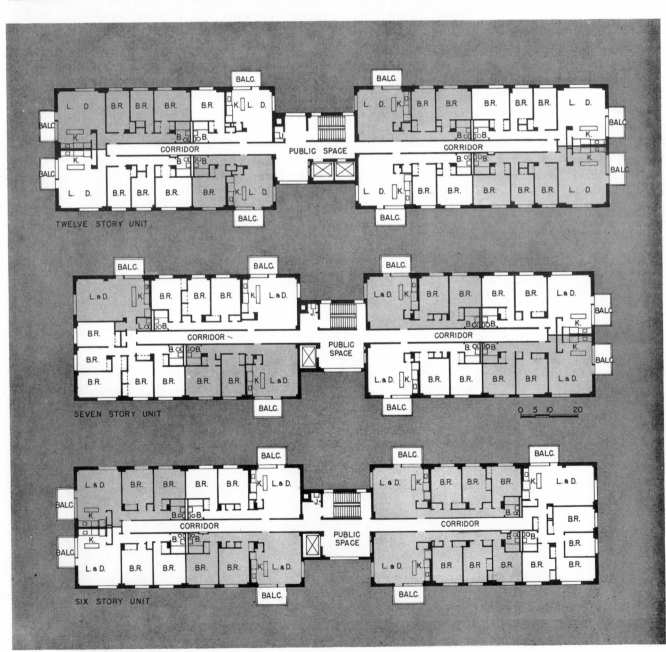

TWELVE STORY UNIT

SEVEN STORY UNIT

0 5 10 20

SIX STORY UNIT

Three basic types of buildings 6, 7 and 12 stories high house 3,070 persons in 704 units apportioned thus:

96	1 BR Unit		13.65%
284	2 BR Units		40.30%
276	3 BR Units		39.30%
36	4 BR Units		5.13%
12	5 BR Units		1.72%

The average dwelling unit contains 4.91 rooms, including 2.42 bedrooms. The project has fulfilled income expectation; has maintained a long waiting list since completion. Bids were received in the spring of 1950; the cost was about $4.65 per sq ft. No unusual methods or materials were possible under the PHA regulations so economies were sought through planning rather than by other and less orthodox means.

Plaget Studios

THE H. C.
PRICE
TOWER

Architect: Frank Lloyd Wright

General Contractor:
Haskell Culwell Construction Co.

Mechanical Engineer:
Collins and Gould

Electrical Engineer:
L. B. Perkins Co.

FRANK LLOYD WRIGHT

Architect of the Tower

THIS GENTLE SKYSCRAPER has escaped the big city to live in an American town in the country . . . To stand there in its own park, casting its own shadow upon its own ground. Reflected in a long slender pool it affords everyone everywhere in it a beautiful view of the rolling countryside that is Oklahoma.

The "skyscraper" in itself, where there is space, is a proper American circumstance; a triumph, not of landlordism, but of our own best technology. It should be a triumph of our architectural artistry as well. But such is not the case. The skyscraper of the big city where skyscrapers crowd upon skyscrapers is a rank weed in what otherwise might be a wholesome garden. The American skyscraper belongs, rather, to our smaller American towns like Bartlesville, where there is still a chance for the spirit of man to live and express itself in a free community that offers a better future to American democracy. The big city of today is servile and doomed by the eternal law of change.

This instance of the tall building in the country now seems to me to be one proper step on the way toward the inevitable, planned-decentralization of the giant-city: the city — a greedy monster — now being undermined by its own extravagance. The unplanned nature of this overgrown old pattern of the city — now so overcrammed with mechanized merchandise — is being accelerated to extinction by its own contrivances. This old pattern is not for the modern free-world of democracy.

Look at this American skyscraper now upright in the American countryside. A natural! Its glass is protected by wide projecting copper blades (or blinds) and tinted gold. The occupant is not only protected against actinic exposure; the whole building is itself shielded against weather. This copper shielding is for the liberation, comfort, and pleasure of those who live and work in the building. Glass is here a blessing to the occupants. Glass, the modern miracle, used *according to human nature*. That would mean used with architectural artistry.

Why not American buildings now as spirited as Mont St. Michel yet as scientific and utilitarian in nature as the automobile, the steamship, or the airplane?

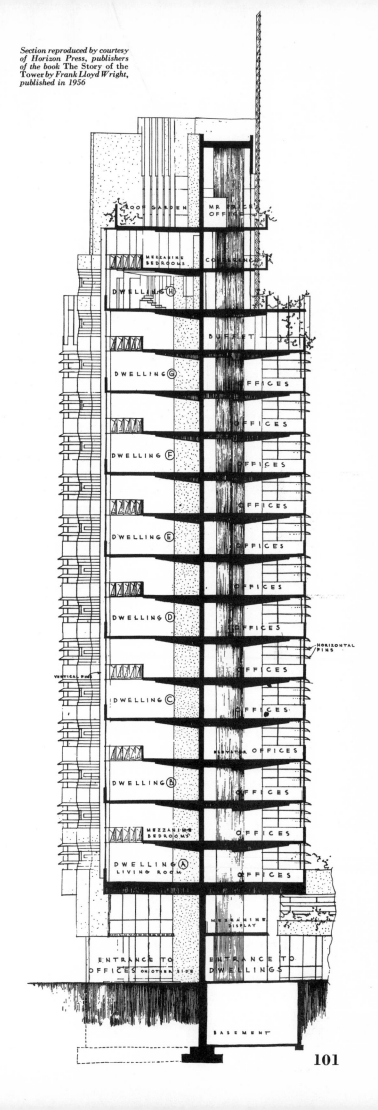

Section reproduced by courtesy of Horizon Press, publishers of the book The Story of the Tower by Frank Lloyd Wright, published in 1956

101

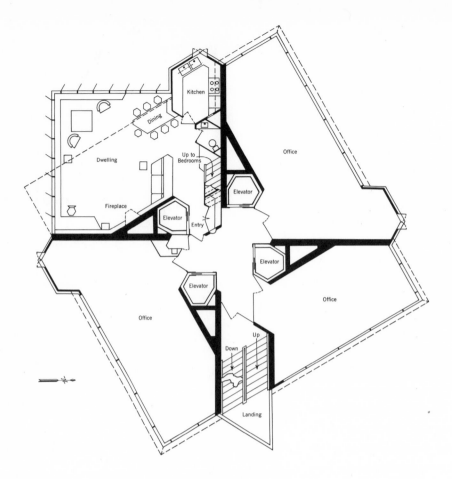

A typical floor of the Price Tower. The unusual combination of offices and apartments in the same building permits around-the-clock use of central facilities and utilities, thus making the structure operate more efficiently. The city of Bartlesville is also provided with more spacious accommodations than had heretofore been available. Mr. Price keeps one apartment for use by out-of-town customers. The other apartments are rented, some to businessmen and professionals who also maintain their offices on the same floor

HAROLD C. PRICE

*Owner of the Tower and
head of the H. C. Price Company:*

THE DECISION to engage Frank Lloyd Wright as the architect for an office building for the H. C. Price Company was prompted by our belief in his ability to create for us and our community a structure of great and lasting beauty.

We were of the opinion that an office building could be made beautiful without affecting its proper functioning. It seemed to us that nearly all office buildings have followed a stereotyped design — with variations — though many have proven very impressive upon completion.

It was not our intent to build a monument. We simply wanted a functional office building that would possess a natural beauty brought about through outstanding design. We wanted a building of which our city would be proud. We believe that we have obtained the desired result.

Working with Mr. Wright and his Fellowship over a period of three years has been a liberal education in the appreciation of the arts of decorative and functional design.

During the construction of a building, the client and Mr. Wright do not always agree. When Frank Lloyd Wright is certain he is correct, he objects to change. But, if the client has logic in his argument, Frank Lloyd Wright will readily consider any sensible changes suggested.

We particularly noted that Mr. Wright is never bound by his original ideas. He will make changes as the work progresses, whenever it is practicable and advantageous to do so. And, without a single exception, during the construction of the Price Tower, every such change that was made resulted in marked improvement.

Joe D: Price

Joe D. Price, *son of the owner;*
who took the photographs:

WHEN ONLY the bare structural form of the building had been erected, it possessed a basic poetry different from the rhythm of the ordinary post and beam and slab system — a beauty that was actually built in before the exterior was ever applied. The outer surfacing — when it was finally fixed in place — merely intensified the ingrained charm and grace of the basic form; a quality best described by Mr. Wright's own term "organic."

When the windows were added to the skeleton, their big mullions tended to make the building appear heavy. This discouraging stage of construc-

tion lasted several months. But one day, when the louvers had been applied to the upper third of the tower, I was walking along Bartlesville's main street and looked up over the little box-type buildings all about me to find the Price building towering majestically over them. Then, for the first time, the true building itself became visible to me. There are no words to describe the intense feeling it gave me. Since then the building has grown in magnitude. As you drive through Bartlesville, down streets, past houses, through alleys, you keep seeing glimpses of the tower rising and thrusting nobly above the rooftops. Everywhere one goes he is aware of it — as a medieval cathedral, it dominates the town.

EDGAR KAUFMANN, JR.

Historian, author, critic:

THE PRICE TOWER culminates an extraordinary tradition that began in 1873 when Frank Lloyd Wright was four years old. Then Frederick Baumann published a pamphlet, *The Art of Preparing Foundations for all Kinds of Buildings with particular Illustrations of the "Method of Isolated Piers" as followed in Chicago.* At eighteen Wright went to work for Adler and Sullivan in the Borden Block, one of the earliest tall buildings erected on isolated piers, and designed by the partners themselves in 1880. Similar piers supported Sullivan's later masterwork, the Wainwright Building. Wright wrote, "As he threw the 'stretch' on my desk with the first three bays outlined in pencil I sensed what had happened . . . Until Louis Sullivan showed the way, high buildings lacked unity. They were built up in layers . . . All except one . . . Root's Monadnock . . . a noble building."

In 1890, tall buildings achieved their first symbolic and purely exterior expressions of unity: the second Leiter building (structurally advanced); the Monadnock (structurally retrogressive); the brilliant Wainwright (structurally symbolic rather than directly expressive). Ever since, unity of surface has remained the admired expression of tall building design.

Baumann's seed idea of the isolated pier was to yield a second harvest, however. In 1929 Wright, after his great skyscraper projects of 1912 and the early 1920's, grasped the isolated pier as the very core of tall building in his scheme for St. Mark's tower. Developing from a 60 foot wooden windmill he erected for his schoolteacher aunts thirty-five years earlier, this concrete and glass shaft achieved a technical and spatial expression of startling originality. Four separate, symmetrical segments were linked by ribbons of patterned copper; fire-stairs differentiated alternate sides of the building; pointed ribs of concrete, evidence of the mast-like structure, impinged on the sky to top it all.

Twenty years later, in the laboratory tower for S. C. Johnson and Son, Wright gave the isolated pier a yet more forcible expression. One great concrete shaft, sunk deep into the earth, rises to carry work-space cantilevered about it, smoothly sealed in bands of brick and glass; the surface the complete expression of the core.

When Harold Price requested a building combining offices and dwellings, Wright reworked and

refined his original scheme of a tower in quadrants. The proportion of three to one in favor of office space produces an exterior asymmetry of continual, graceful surprises. Fire stairs and core-walls rise to a coronet of offices for the owner. Blue-green copper — inside and out — counters the different blue of the sky; golden glass softens the strong prairie daylight or warms the dusk. Copper fins further modify the light — vertical over the apartment windows, horizontal elsewhere — ensuring in silhouette the vibrant dotted line Wright always prefers. The structural core of the Price Tower effloresces in movement, color, texture, ornament, and (in the penthouse mural) art, all held together and in scale by integration with the structure itself — inner unity and identity here embodied in an architecture that establishes as seldom before a new horizon.

FORDHAM

Bronx, N. Y.

Thomas Airviews Photo

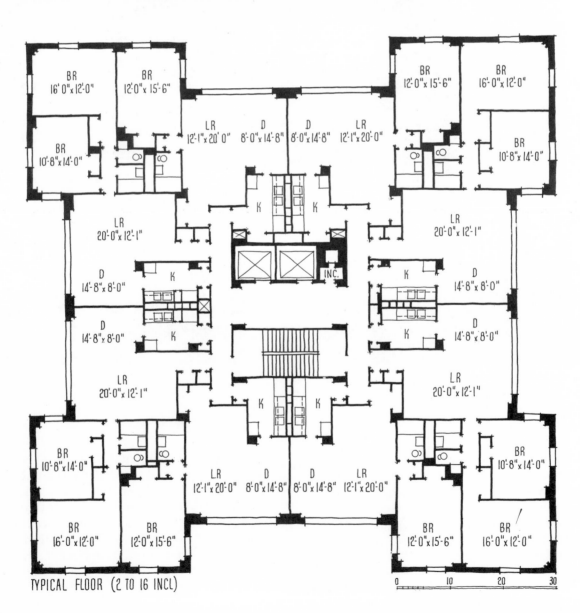

BR 16'-0" x 12'-0"	BR 12'-0" x 15'-6"		BR 12'-0" x 15'-6"	BR 16'-0" x 12'-0"

LR 12'-1" x 20'-0"   D 8'-0" x 14'-8"   D 8'-0" x 14'-8"   LR 12'-1" x 20'-0"

BR 10'-8" x 14'-0"

BR 10'-8" x 14'-0"

LR 20'-0" x 12'-1"

LR 20'-0" x 12'-1"

K   K

INC.

D 14'-8" x 8'-0"   K

K   D 14'-8" x 8'-0"

D 14'-8" x 8'-0"   K

K   D 14'-8" x 8'-0"

LR 20'-0" x 12'-1"

LR 20'-0" x 12'-1"

K   K

K   K

BR 10'-8" x 14'-0"

BR 10'-8" x 14'-0"

LR 12'-1" x 20'-0"   D 8'-0" x 14'-8"   D 8'-0" x 14'-8"   LR 12'-1" x 20'-0"

BR 16'-0" x 12'-0"   BR 12'-0" x 15'-6"

BR 12'-0" x 15'-6"   BR 16'-0" x 12'-0"

TYPICAL FLOOR (2 TO 16 INCL)

0   10   20   30

HILL APARTMENTS

Leonard Schultze and Associates, Architects

Joseph Molitor Photos

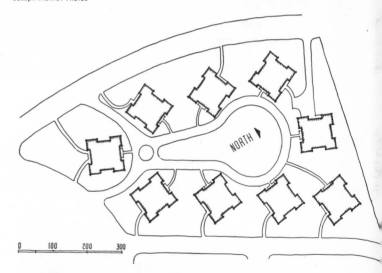

ALL TOO rare, in recent years of federalized apartment planning, are projects conceived like Fordham Hill. This huge apartment development was chosen for presentation here as a current example of long-term investment of life insurance funds, planned without much concern over current excitements, either economic or stylistic, but representing the collective opinion of an imposing aggregation of planners all looking toward the future. The owners (Equitable Life Assurance Society), the architects (Leonard Schultze & Associates), the consultants (City Investing Company) and the builders (Starrett Bros. and Eken) all got into discussions of such questions as tall vs. low buildings, inside or outside kitchens, trying to chart the course of apartment living in the years ahead.

There will undoubtedly be lifted eyebrows over the concept of nine 16-story buildings housing 1118 families on a single site. Advocate of the height was Robert W. Dowling (City Investing) who can't abide the idea of spending one's hard-earned leisure in commuting to the country.

The fact is that Fordham Hill splits the difference; it is in the Bronx, a short commuting ride by subway or train from the city. It is out of the canyons of Manhattan, where views from the upper stories include the rivers, the Sound, the Palisades. There is another reason for the height — distant views dispel the ground-level sense of congestion.

Cost is a cogent argument for height. Land cost, to be sure, in the large city. But more significantly, the long-term cost of maintenance. Metropolitan Life is said, for example, to find operating costs 25 per cent higher in low buildings than in high. That is why Parkmerced, at San Francisco, is being finished with high buildings after being started with low ones.

Another major decision at Fordham Hill was to use the interior kitchen. Starting with the fact that frozen foods and such have freed the housewife from long hours in the kitchen, Fordham Hill uses the inside kitchen, mechanically ventilated, to open a wide combination of living and dining space to views through extensive windows. The ventilation flow, it is pointed out also, is in the right direction; kitchen fans pull outside air into the apartment, into the kitchen, and up the stack. With an outside kitchen, any ventilation is likely to pull kitchen odors into the apartment.

Beyond that Fordham Hill's rooms are of generous proportion — quite large for mass housing. This is one of its best assurances of continued popularity through the years.

Fordham Hill represents the high-building concept of apartment planning — save cost and
commuting time for tenants, make the development large enough to establish its own neighborhood, bring the gardens and playgrounds to
the city dweller, don't send the people out to
the gardens. Large rooms and wide windows,
high in air, open apartments to distant views

Joseph Molitor Photos

The interior kitchen has its share in the opening of apartments to views; it permits a wide combination of living and dining space, with a long strip of windows. The rooms are of generous size in the first place, and with the linear arrangement of added dining space along the outer wall, the living area becomes something really spacious. Buildings are oriented on the site so that one does not block views from another; fortunately there are good scenic possibilities in several different directions

LONG ISLAND: STATE-AIDED SUBURBAN HOUSING

Harbor Homes, Port Washington, L. I.,and Spinney Hill Homes, Manhasset, L. I.

William Lescaze, Architect   *Claude R. Engle, Electrical Engineer*

Leo A. Novick, Landscape Architect   *Morris Shapiro, Mechanical Engineer*

IN THESE PROJECTS, plot coverage is low (13 and 16 per cent), the buildings are judiciously placed among trees and planting, residential scale is emphasized both by the 2-story height and the fire-wall projections at 65-ft intervals. A restful horizontal line is created and carried through all the houses by the device of covering the second floor exterior with redwood siding in contrast to the brick below. The foregoing are some of the factors that lend these 2-story row houses their pleasingly residential character. The projects are designed for low-income families and are located on Long Island's north shore; were made possible by a combination of local and state funds.

In executing such a project, the first action comes from the local group (in this case the North Hempstead Housing Authority), which is, of course, acutely aware of the need and makes application to the New York State Division of Housing for assistance. The State agency then surveys the situation, verifies the need, and sets up a tentative proposal according to their standards

Joseph W. Molitor

and procedures. Should the two concepts be at variance, the differences are mutually adjusted, agreement reached, and the State is then prepared to lend assistance. There must be a local contribution (usually restricted by the legal limits on borrowing) to which is added the State aid, which assumes the form of part loan, part subsidy. The project then moves ahead, mostly under local supervision, with consultation and advice from the State agency, and with certain approvals required.

Two to three years ago, when these projects were built, the policy was to keep rentals below $9 per room per month, based upon units averaging 4.2 rooms or less which cost approximately $10,000, excluding landscaping but including a proportionate share of the community building. In general terms, these figures were substantially maintained in these particular setups.

There are a total of 168 units in the two projects; 102 in Spinney Hill and 66 in Harbor Homes. The units range from 3½ to 6½ rooms, a large percentage being 4½ rooms; the density per acre is 58 persons in 14 units at Spinney Hill and 49 persons in 11.8 units at Harbor Homes. The project is designed for families which range from middling to large in size.

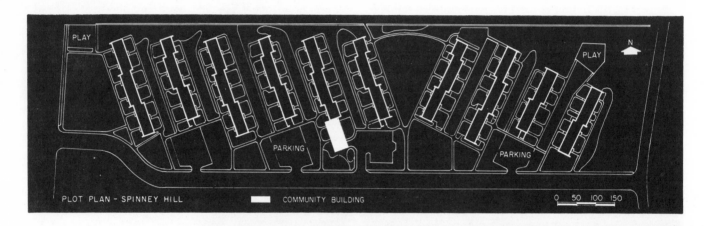

The plot plans — Spinney Hill above, Harbor Homes at right — show the relationship of the houses to lawns, play spaces, drying yards, parking areas, and the community building

The alternate arrangements possible within the repeated module of the fire-wall divisions are shown in the unit plans, right. Note how, for economy, plumbing is back-to-back in plan; also "stacked" vertically

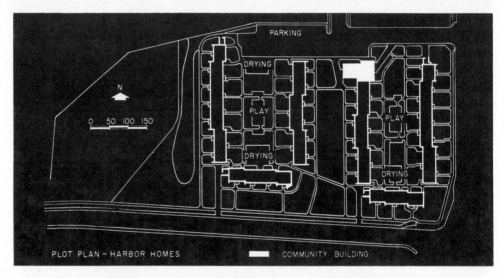

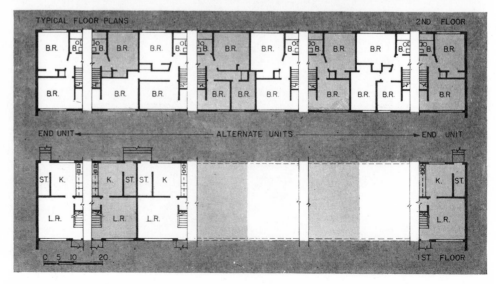

Joseph W. Molitor

113

HOUSING PROJECT AVOIDS FREIGHT-YARD LOOK

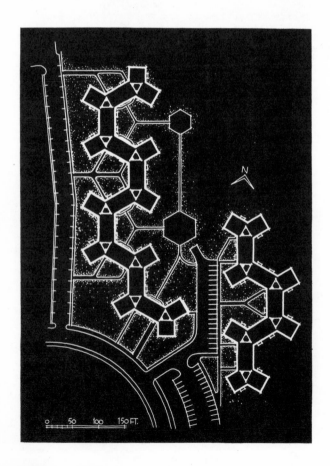

WANTING especially in this instance to avoid the usual slummy associations of a public housing project, the architect worked to develop something better than the customary freight-yard disposition of buildings. The scheme of radiating elements on a 120-degree arc lends interest and variety, also conserves on the number of stairs required for exits. The device also prevents apartments from looking directly at others, gives a wider angle of view, and creates courts of different shapes and sizes.

Basements had to be eliminated because of water conditions; hence, at alternating entrances, utility rooms and laundries are placed on the ground floor. Passages through the building give access to play spaces in the center of the project without the necessity of crossing any streets. Each apartment has direct access to laundry and incinerator in stair hall; each also has its own storage room within the apartment.

Buildings are fire-resistant, with masonry walls and center columns and concrete floors; heating from a central plant.

State Aided Veterans' Housing, Chelsea, Mass.

Hugh Stubbins, Jr., Architect

Thos. Worcester, Inc., Engineers

Chambers & Morice,

Landscape Architects and Site Planners

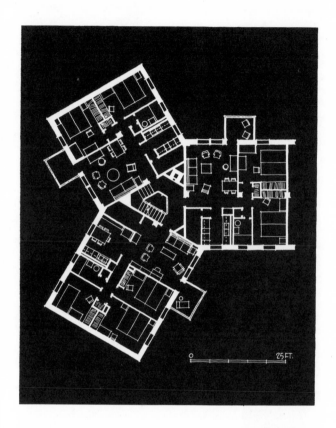

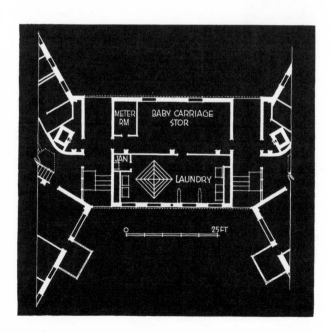

115

Hedrich-Blessing Photos

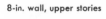
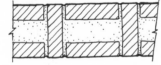

10½-in. wall, first story

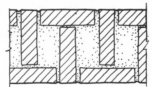

Unique reinforced rowlock brick construction pioneered by Holsman, Holsman, Klekamp & Taylor at Lunt-Lake Apartments. Every other brick is set in rowlock fashion as a wall tie. Wall is reinforced with two ½-in. vertical rods 24 in o.c. and two ⅜-in. horizontal rods in every third course; then wall is made monolithic by pouring grout to fill interstices. This system is said to have saved cost and erection time, by permitting a third more wall area to be laid up per mason-day. The wall is both load-bearing and curtain, saves exterior columns and spandrels

Copyright 1950 by F. W. Dodge Corporation

LUNT-LAKE APARTMENTS, CHICAGO

Pace Associates

Holsman, Holsman, Klekamp & Taylor

Frank J. Kornacker

Associated Architects and Engineers

IN MAN's constant effort to find ways to live in a large city, Chicago is currently much in the news for apartment innovations of considerable variety. There seems to be an unusual willingness to accept the apartment way of life as a permanent situation, not merely as a stop-gap to the home in the suburbs. Maybe it's the spatial vastness of Chicago (shades of Daniel Burnham!) or maybe it's the great lake front. At any rate a large number of Chicago people seem willing to invest in cooperative apartments and settle down in a large building. Thus Chicago, perhaps more than any other city, is building family-size apartment units, as against the ubiquitous efficiency unit.

Lunt-Lake is a more than usually interesting example of Chicago's current crop of mutual ownership buildings. Its apartments, while not mansions, all have two or three bedrooms, lots and lots of closet and storage space, open outlooks toward the lake view, and economical construction. Its reinforced rowlock brick construction is unique (see opposite page). And it uses an economical system of floor slabs and concrete block partitions to save construction cost and cubage.

This floor system consists of prefabricated 16-ga metal box joists with reinforcing steel pre-set into the box, and 3-in. lightweight precast slabs grouted in place after assembly. The system keeps story height to 8 ft 4 in., and permits a four-story walkup with virtually no more steps than in the once-prevalent three-story-English-basement type of building.

One of Lunt-Lake's three buildings is a four-story walkup; the other two are nine-story elevator buildings. The top floor of the walkup building adds compensation for the extra climb with studio-type suites with sloping ceilings following a ridge-type roof, and open fireplaces. All other apartments have the floor joists and precast slabs exposed; partitions are of exposed, painted concrete block, 4 by 12 by 3½ in.

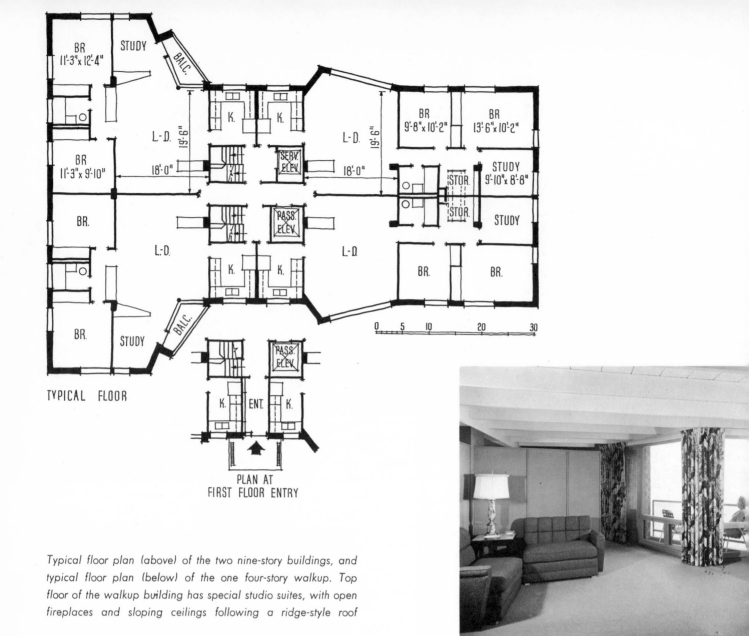

BR
11'-3"x 12'-4"

STUDY

BALC.

K.

K.

L-D.

19'-6"

L-D.

19'-6"

BR
9'-8"x 10'-2"

BR
13'-6"x 10'-2"

18'-0"

BR
11'-3"x 9'-10"

SERV.
ELEV.

18'-0"

STUDY
9'-10"x 8'-8"

STOR.

STUDY

BR.

PASS.
ELEV.

L-D.

L-D.

STOR.

BR.

L-D.

BR.

BR.

STUDY

BALC.

0   5   10   20   30

TYPICAL FLOOR

K.   ENT.   K.

PASS.
ELEV.

PLAN AT
FIRST FLOOR ENTRY

Typical floor plan (above) of the two nine-story buildings, and typical floor plan (below) of the one four-story walkup. Top floor of the walkup building has special studio suites, with open fireplaces and sloping ceilings following a ridge-style roof

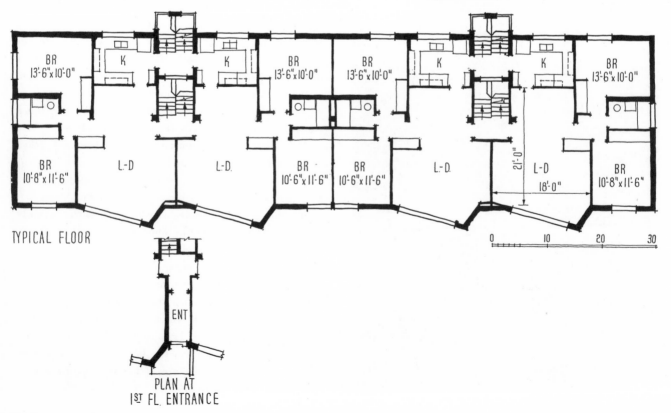

BR
13'-6"x 10'-0"

K

K

BR
13'-6"x 10'-0"

BR
13'-6"x 10'-0"

K

K

BR
13'-6"x 10'-0"

BR
10'-8"x 11'-6"

L-D

L-D

BR
10'-6"x 11'-6"

BR
10'-6"x 11'-6"

L-D

21'-0"

L-D

BR
10'-8"x 11'-6"

18'-0"

TYPICAL FLOOR

0   10   20   30

ENT

PLAN AT
1ST FL. ENTRANCE

Hedrich-Blessing Photos

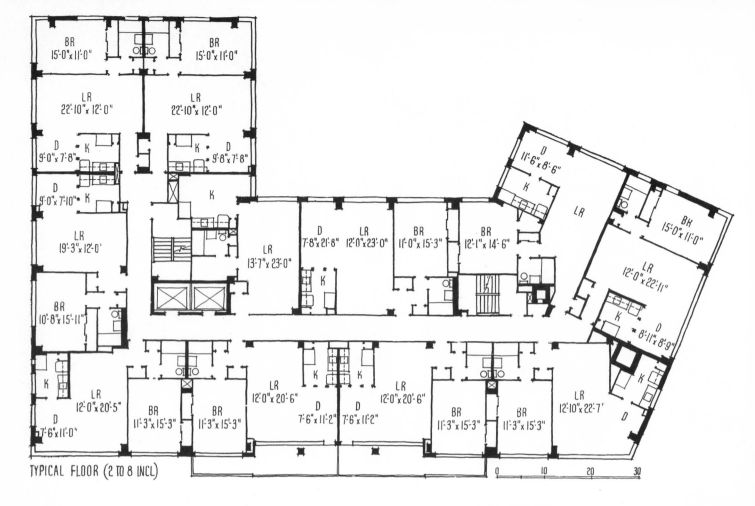

TYPICAL FLOOR (2 TO 8 INCL)

0   10   20   30

CRESTVIEW APARTMENTS

Wisconsin Avenue, Washington, D. C.

Berla & Abel, Architects

Otto Vogt, Structural Engineer

General Engineering Associates, Mechanical Engineers

THIS building reverses the field of 608 apartment layout — instead of the usual high proportion of no-bedroom units, it has 77 units with bedrooms, only 11 "efficiency" suites. And it goes against the tide also in offering larger than usual rooms. Thus it offers more commodious living, and is expected to have long-term competitive advantage over the many, many 608 buildings now coming into the Washington market.

Parking space was obtained under the rear portion of the building by leaving columns exposed and omitting exterior walls. Ceilings over this space are heated to prevent cold floors above. A fenced-in roof deck above the eighth floor provides the tenants a place for sun bathing or a cool spot to sit on a summer evening.

120   CRESTVIEW

Here too (see also p. 107) the device of the inside kitchen, with mechanical ventilation, is used to add spaciousness at the windows. Combined living and dining space, facing outward through wide strip windows, is quite pleasant, and the views are good, for the site is unusually high

MINIMUM-HOUSEKEEPI

Most apartments face north or south (below
and left); those on east have balconies.
Only windows on west are in stair well

Copyright 1953 by F. W. Dodge Corporation

APARTMENTS ON DOWNTOWN SITE

Walter Bragg Smith Apartments, Montgomery, Alabama

THIS TWELVE-STORY APARTMENT HOUSE, only two blocks from downtown Montgomery, was planned primarily for business men and women. Of its 122 apartments, 103 are single-room minimum-housekeeping "studios" and 19 are one-bedroom suites.

In plan the building is L-shaped to overcome the difficulties of a limited and sharply sloping site, facilitate on-site parking, and provide the maximum number of apartments on the north side facing a panoramic view of the city. While the steepness of the site necessitated extensive excavation and a high retaining wall to make the space between the south wall and the edge of the lot usable as a driveway, it also permitted inclusion of a mezzanine over half the lobby floor.

The building, entirely financed through the FHA, is an outstanding example of what can be done architecturally under the restrictions imposed by the housing law; it won the Honor Award at the Third Annual Gulf States Regional Conference last October. Framing is steel, floors are 2-in. concrete slab. End walls are gray face brick, spandrels are green glazed tile, columns are faced with mosaic tile. Italian marble is used on the exterior of the first floor and in the lobby. The building is fully air conditioned.

Main entrances are on north (above and below) and east (top, opposite); both lead directly to lobby. Parking area is at west

Lobby area is more like that of residential hotel than an apartment house, includes registration and mail desk, lounge, newsstand, and public rest rooms. Mural is air view of entire city; walls around entrance are Italian marble; floors are terrazzo

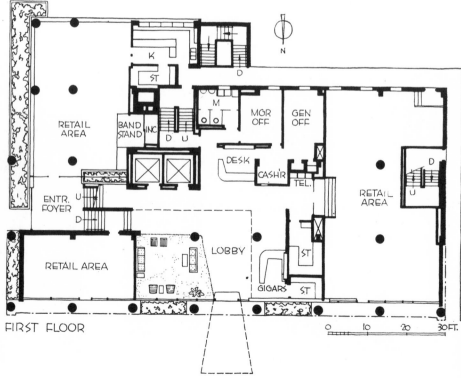

FIRST FLOOR

Photographer's studio (left and below), dress shop and drug store are current occupants of ground-floor retail areas. Owner required maximum retail space on lobby floor, got three separate areas each with street frontage, lobby access

Joseph W. Molitor

MEZZANINE FLOOR

Mezzanine, made possible by sharp slope of site, extends over western half of lobby floor, houses rest room and lounge and four apartments. East entrance to building is on intermediate level, has own small lobby with stairs leading up to mezzanine and down to main north lobby

Upper floors have 11 studio and two one-bedroom apartments each, arranged to permit creation of larger suites (bottom of page) with minimum of structural change. Aluminum sun shades (above) protect south windows. Utility elements—baths, kitchens, etc.—are grouped around pipe chases

TYPICAL FLOOR

0 10 20 30 FT.

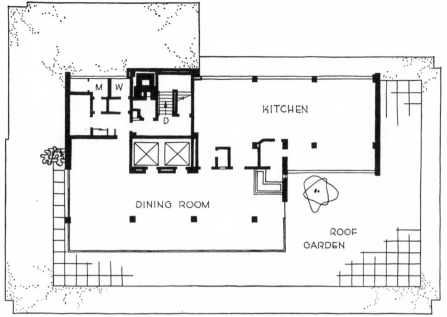

PENT HOUSE

Penthouse, originally planned as cocktail lounge and private-party area, was rented as restaurant after construction was well under way; plans had to be revised to provide much larger kitchen and dining space. Restaurant is open to public, has spectacular view, and is one of city's best

Joseph W. Molitor

HOUSING FOR THE UNITED STATES EMBASSY

F. Murasawa

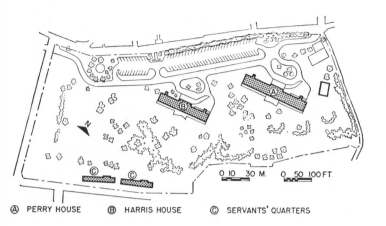

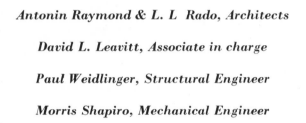

Antonin Raymond & L. L Rado, Architects

David L. Leavitt, Associate in charge

Paul Weidlinger, Structural Engineer

Morris Shapiro, Mechanical Engineer

STAFF IN TOKYO, JAPAN

Favorably located on a hill and oriented south for view, sun and breeze, these are the first true multi-story reinforced concrete structures in Tokyo — the conventional system being a concrete covered light steel frame. On poor bearing and tall for Japan, the structural design had to cope with seismic forces. The solution is a series of box frames formed by the through party walls which support the floor system. Acting as cantilevers six to seven floors high, the frames serve both as shear walls resisting lateral shock and as support against longitudinal vibration. The horizontal ribs support the floors and become also a stiffening membrane. Under vibration tests simulating earthquake conditions, the building exhibited favorable dynamic characteristics.

The section at right shows the overall organization of the six floors, in which the top four are devoted principally to duplexes, as described more fully on the following pages. Each apartment has a terrace facing south, separated from its neighbors by gaily colored dividing screens.

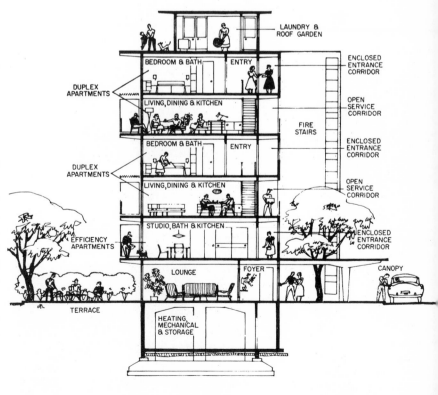

129

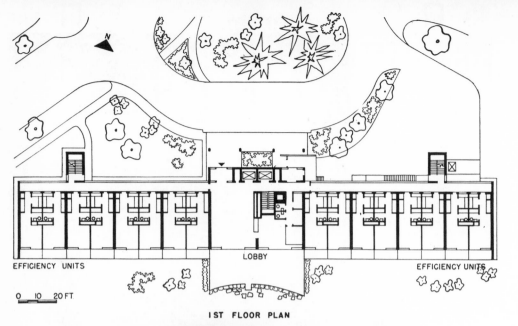

EFFICIENCY UNITS   EFFICIENCY UNITS

0   10   20 FT

1ST FLOOR PLAN

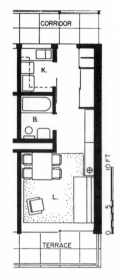

CORRIDOR

K.

B.

L.

TERRACE

EFFICIENCY UNIT

*First floor, plan at left, is devoted to
efficiency units, as is the second. Planned
for bachelor occupants, the units contain
a living-sleeping room, kitchen and bath.
Photo at left shows the convertible bed
unit, which was, as all the furniture,
designed by the architects for manufacture in Japan*

SINGLE BEDROOM UNIT

*The lower two photos at left and plan
below show the single bedroom unit,
which is located in the central two bays,
above the lobby, on all floors. The sliding
door between bedroom and living room
provides daytime openness and night-
time privacy. Wall finishes for all apartments are largely of plywood*

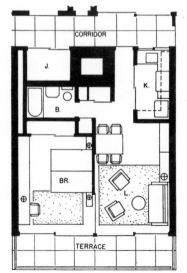

CORRIDOR

J.   K.

B.

BR.   L.

TERRACE

F. Murasawa

130   EMBASSY HOUSING, TOKYO

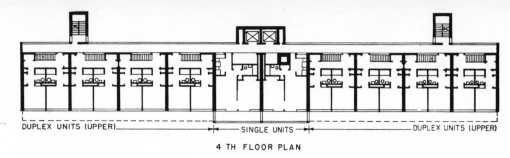

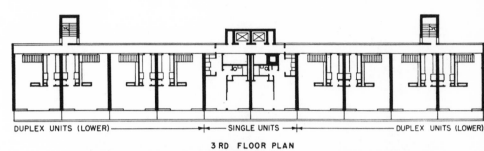

CORRIDOR

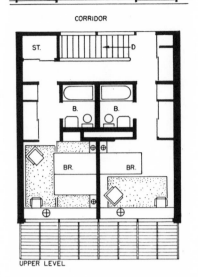

UPPER LEVEL

4 TH FLOOR PLAN

DUPLEX UNITS (UPPER) — SINGLE UNITS — DUPLEX UNITS (UPPER)

3 RD FLOOR PLAN

DUPLEX UNITS (LOWER) — SINGLE UNITS — DUPLEX UNITS (LOWER)

DUPLEX UNIT

Unusual duplex apartments occupy the third to sixth floors, plans above, except for the single bedroom units in the center bays. Tenant entrance is from an enclosed corridor at upper level, plan above, so that bedrooms may be entered without disturbing the living area, and also to separate servant and occupant traffic. The open servants' gallery at lower level, plan below, provides entrance and delivery into the kitchen and cross ventilation for this level. Flexibility which yields units ranging from one to four bedrooms in size has been ingeniously furnished. By removing knockout panels and adding doors, see plan, bedrooms can be added or subtracted almost at will

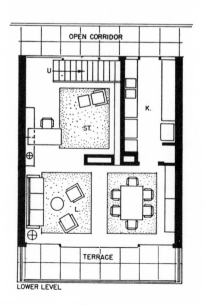

LOWER LEVEL

Prairie Avenue Courts, Chicago

For Chicago Housing Authority

George Fred Keck — William Keck, Architects

Samuel R. Lewis & Associates, Mechanical Engineers

Frank J. Kornacker & Associates, Structural Engineers

W. G. Atkinson, Landscape Architect

Hedrich-Blessing

ARCHITECTURAL CONCEPTS OF HOUSING PROVED VALID

As PUBLIC HOUSING this project has won enthusiastic kudos. Observers stress the avoidance of a standard type of building, with standardized units and thus standardized occupants. In the variety of buildings — fourteen-story, seven-story and two-story apartments and row houses — there is a variety of accommodations, ranging from one to four bedrooms. Automatically then the project attracts diversified family groups and has a natural and stable neighborhood cohesion.

These facts alone would be sufficient to earn for it a high rating among public housing projects, but architects will be quick to note attractive concomitants. The variety of buildings has much stronger appeal than can be stated in statistics of family groups. It obviates the deadly monotony of so many apartment projects, the filed-away feeling. There is contrast, there is composition, there is form and mass and shadow. There is change in the lawns, playgrounds, parking spaces. If there is economy in the building of it, and there is, there is denial of what Dean Hudnut dubs the "ancient title to dreariness" of housing for the lower income groups.

This achievement was not accomplished without some struggle. There were those who argued against the tall building, others who did not like the row houses. And, no doubt, there were some to whom the mere fact of variety seemed radical. But the architects' persistence was not to be denied, and in the end it makes Prairie Avenue Courts a noteworthy proof of the validity of architectural thinking.

Notice (site plan, next page) that the disposition of buildings follows a shadow pattern. Careful studies were made of sun angles throughout the year to minimize the shading of one building by another. The heaviest shadows fall on the parking lots, the least on the playgrounds and buildings.

The architects explain that the overall pattern of accommodations makes no claim of universal applicability; it was dictated solely by needs of the city's public housing program. A secondary consideration was that there was to be a minimum of dislocation of families during the construction stages. It is important, nevertheless, that the pattern did meet the specifications as to population density.

Economy was a major consideration in design; exclusive of land the average cost per family unit was $8500. The high-rise buildings are of reinforced concrete, with exterior walls of hollow brick and concrete block construction. Low buildings follow the same construction except that walls are load bearing. There are no plaster walls in the project; interior partitions are of lightweight concrete block, painted.

133

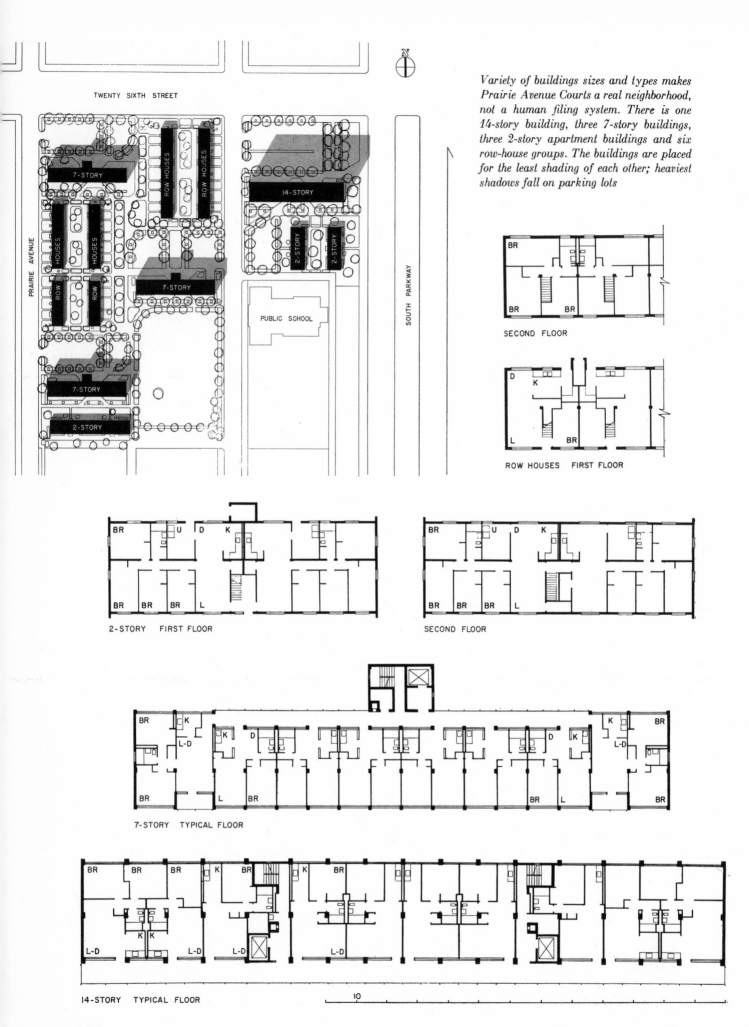

TWENTY SIXTH STREET

7-STORY

ROW HOUSES

ROW HOUSES

14-STORY

PRAIRIE AVENUE

ROW HOUSES

ROW HOUSES

2-STORY

2-STORY

7-STORY

ROW

ROW

SOUTH PARKWAY

7-STORY

PUBLIC SCHOOL

2-STORY

Variety of buildings sizes and types makes Prairie Avenue Courts a real neighborhood, not a human filing system. There is one 14-story building, three 7-story buildings, three 2-story apartment buildings and six row-house groups. The buildings are placed for the least shading of each other; heaviest shadows fall on parking lots

BR

BR

BR

SECOND FLOOR

D   K

L   BR

ROW HOUSES   FIRST FLOOR

BR   U   D   K

BR   BR   BR   L

2-STORY   FIRST FLOOR

BR   U   D   K

BR   BR   BR   L

SECOND FLOOR

BR   K
L-D

BR   L   BR

K   D

K

K   BR
L-D

BR   L   BR

7-STORY   TYPICAL FLOOR

BR   BR   BR   K   BR   K   BR

K   K

L-D   L-D   L-D   L-D

14-STORY   TYPICAL FLOOR

10

IV
Apartments: Small Projects

TWO-STORY TRIPLEX MAKES THE MOST

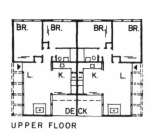

UPPER FLOOR

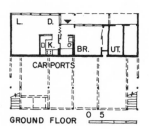

GROUND FLOOR 0 5

Apartment Building, Berkeley, Calif.

Roger Lee, Architect

Hsih Heng Wang, Structural Engineer
A. L. Muzzini, General Contractor

In order to obtain maximum income from a corner plot containing apartments, the owner decided to develop a remaining piece at the rear in two-story units. This small area—60 ft wide and 50 ft deep—gives onto a side street. The neighborhood is an established one near the univer-

OF A SMALL PLOT

sity, and the architect was requested to enliven it by means of an interesting structure in which the units were to be small, informal, and compact—each having an outdoor living area.

City requirements for setbacks and parking made three units possible; the best orientation for privacy and sunshine was to the front or rear. Thus, sun-decks for the upper units were placed toward the front, while a patio-entrance terrace for the lower unit was placed at the rear.

For the exterior, the redwood siding was stained reddish-beige, and the fascias, beams, posts, and trim were stained dark brown. Interior plywood walls are natural mahogany; sliding panels and kitchen appliances are yellow.

The structural frame, sash, and doors are wood, and the ceilings are exposed plank; floors are asphalt-cork tile; heating is by gas-fired wall furnaces.

APARTMENT INNOVATIONS

50 Joice Street Apartments

John E. Kramer, Owner and Contractor

John G. Kelley, Architect

FOR SAN FRANCISCO

Roger Sturtevant Photos

A NARROW San Francisco street tests the ingenuity of an architect fairly severely, but by the same token it becomes a good place to demonstrate that quality. The photograph on the opposite page has a before and after suggestion, with the clean, uncluttered simplicity of modern design together with the efforts of an earlier era. Plan and section below illustrate the ingenuity with which fire escapes were kept inside.

The confines of the site coupled with the financial requirements of the project resulted in several innovations. Separation of the building into two units, each 20 by 60 ft, simplified the construction and provided an interior court for vertical circulation and light. Staggering the floor levels of the two units allowed the stairs to span from one to the other in an economical arrangement. The narrow shape of the units puts the long side of the living room and the bedroom on the open side, with kitchens and baths grouped (for economical plumbing) on the court side. Fire escapes are kept off the front of the building, and serve also for the service entrances.

There is perhaps some incongruity between the message of the photographs and that of the floor plans. The apartments are quite small, due partly to the owner's desire to get in the maximum allowable number of rental units, and partly to the location of the property. Joice Street is close to downtown San Francisco, and has a sort of gentle Bohemian character which makes it a logical place for the junior executive or the career girl. Nobody imagines the building appealing to families with children, or even with any accumulation of bulky possessions. In other words the logical tenants find in this building a combination of visual appeal and compact convenience which should make this project pay out rather nicely.

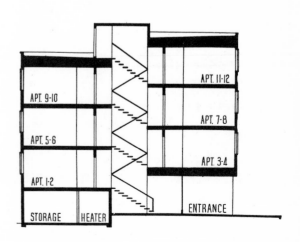

The 50 Joice Street Apartments are of wood frame construction, with stained redwood exterior. Interior walls are of integral color plaster. Windows, both fixed and casement, are of wood. Walls between apartments are double, with acoustic insulation between

WINDSWEPT APARTMENTS, MIAMI

Robert Law Weed and Associates

Architects—Engineers

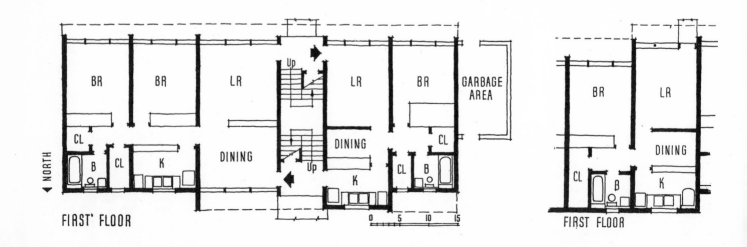

BR   BR   LR

Up

LR   BR   GARBAGE AREA

CL

CL   B   CL   K

DINING

DINING

CL   B

K

Up

NORTH

FIRST FLOOR

0   5   10   15

BR   LR

CL

DINING

B   K

FIRST FLOOR

HERE is another of the many current apartment buildings which gave the architects some problems in making something attractive in small room sizes. If you consider these rooms quite small — and the architects do — they are still "somewhat larger than permitted under the then existing FHA criteria." Nevertheless this building has strong appeal for its intended tenants, young business people who want a near-downtown location rather than extensive housekeeping. Moreover, the apartments were furnished by the owner (George Farkas designed the interiors), so it was possible to control the scale of the rooms.

Perhaps the nicest feature — and the one which gives the buildings their character — is the provision for cross ventilation. The large awning-type windows make the rooms truly "windswept" and the projected overhangs above protect the windows not only from sun but also from the sudden downpours which the Miami chamber of commerce doesn't deny. Thus people who are away all day may leave windows open without too much concern for the rain.

Good storage space is another feature worthy of note. This may be, as the architects suggest, an especial need in Florida, but even in the cold north tenants seem to appreciate huge closets for extra things, and full-wall cabinets to bedrooms.

Buildings are of reinforced concrete column and beam construction. First floor is a slab on fill, second floor a light slab on precast concrete joists. Exterior walls are of concrete block with painted concrete surfacing. Interior walls are of sand finish plaster. Windows are wood, with inside screens and Venetian blinds.

Ezra Stoller: Pictor

Julius Shulman Photos

EL-KAY APARTMENTS

Westwood, Los Angeles

Richard J. Neutra, Architect

HERE is a deliberate attempt to give the rented build-ing the qualities of the individual home. Firstly, the building is designed to age inconspicuously. Secondly, it provides outdoor space, with foliage for both screening and view, and maximum size is al-lotted to living and social quarters, extending where possible into decks or patios. Stylistically the building is to please a diversified tenancy, without the ear-marks of fashion and date. So here is an excellent ex-ample of a residential concept of apartment dwelling, nicely freed from the regimented aspect so generally associated with apartment house design.

Copyright 1958 by F. W. Dodge Corporation

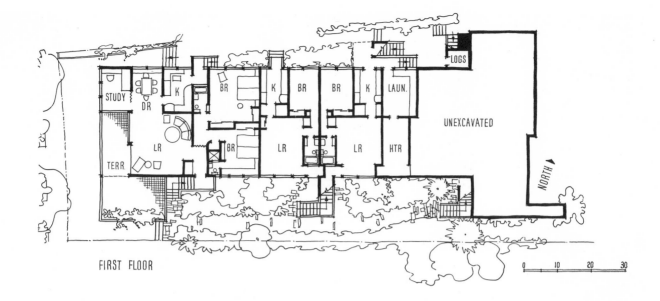

FIRST FLOOR

STUDY · DR · K · BR · K · BR · BR · K · LAUN. · LOGS

LR · BR · LR · LR · HTR

TERR.

UNEXCAVATED

NORTH

0 10 20 30

Construction is a timber chassis with fire-resistant cement plaster. Large view windows of plate glass, steel sash, sliding doors, insulated roof. Many apartments have blond paneling of unselected birch; living areas are carpeted for the tenants

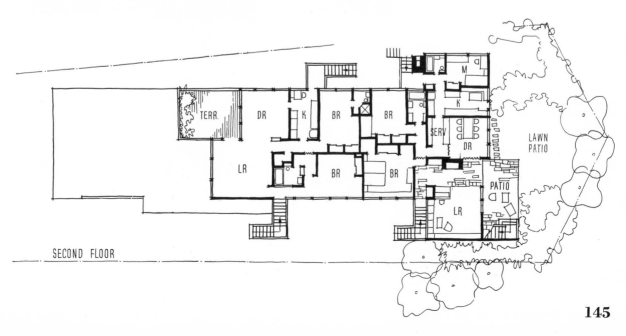

SECOND FLOOR

TERR. · DR · K · BR · BR · M · K · SERV · DR · LAWN PATIO

LR · BR · BR · PATIO · LR

145

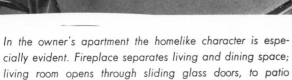

In the owner's apartment the homelike character is especially evident. Fireplace separates living and dining space; living room opens through sliding glass doors, to patio

Julius Shulman Photos

Some apartments have outdoor living rooms in patios at ground level; others have elevated deck terraces as the hilly site was developed to utilize outdoor stairs as screens for little private gardens

TWO-FAMILY HOUSE WITH A DIFFERENCE—PRIVACY

House for Mr. and Mrs. Walter Costa

Lafayette, Calif.

Walter Costa, Architect

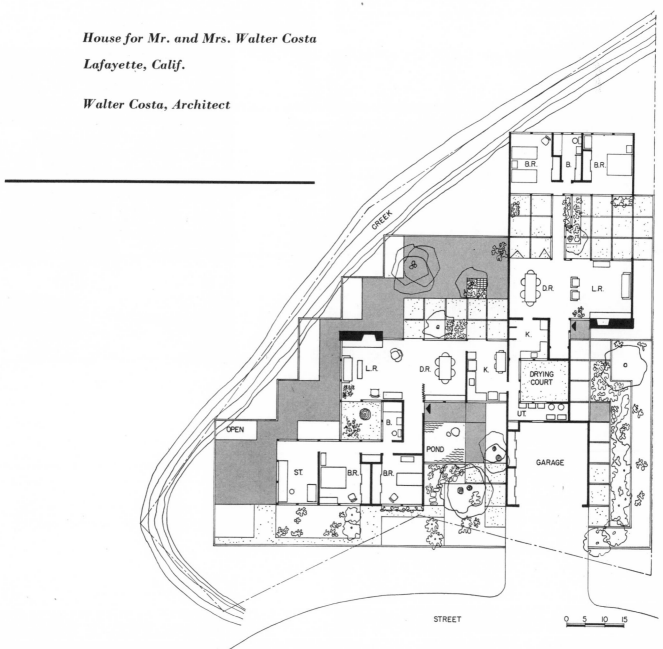

Tʜᴇ ʀᴇᴀsᴏɴ ʜᴇ ʙᴜɪʟᴛ ᴀ ᴅᴜᴘʟᴇx, Architect Walter Costa explains, is that the kind of house he and his wife wanted would not have been economically feasible without the income-producing rental unit.

The site they selected, not far outside San Francisco, was ideal for the purpose — handy to shopping, schools and transportation, almost wholly level, and triangular in shape with a brook running along the long leg. A dozen or more fine old oak trees, one of which the house literally was built around, and the location of the brook "presented the greatest challenge," the architect says "and were the primary influence on the building design."

As the plot plan on the preceding page shows, the triangularity of the lot was used to separate the two units as much as possible. Each of the two has two bedrooms, one bath, living dining space and kitchen, and the owners' also has a combination studio and sewing room. Laundry, utility room and garage are common to the two units. A long, roof-height redwood wall with only one opening (a door from the owners' kitchen to the utility room) separates the two and gives each an unusual amount of privacy.

The basis of the design, the architect says, was "to employ an inexpensive structural system and inexpensive materials, but to use them to their best advantage and use the funds available to acquire as much space as possible, arranged as interestingly as possible." Since the site was virtually flat, a concrete slab floor with colored cement finish was used except in the bedroom wing of the rental unit which has a wood floor, cantilevered over the creek. A 5 ft 4 in. modular grid was used with post and lintel framing and joist roof construction. Interior walls and ceilings are finished in ¼-in. hardboard with ¼-in. open joints between sheets; this made an inexpensive surface for painting, and the open joints created a paneled appearance which will not show cracked joints when settlement occurs. Exterior finish is glass, 1 by 6 redwood T&G applied vertically, or ½-in. waterproof plywood.

Entrance to owners' unit is through a landscaped court, along a covered walk and past a pool with an oriental lantern in one corner. The huge oak tree — 40 ft high, trunk diameter 3½ ft — around which house was built has its own glass-walled patio off living room (above right, and bottom opposite). Living-dining room and kitchen open to deck at rear, shielded by roof-high redwood fence

Dining area walls are less than ceiling height, increasing sense of spaciousness and improving both light and ventilation. Main entrance bypasses this area, leads almost directly to living room; rear terrace is visible from just inside door. In order to use part of lot sloping down to creek bed, an extensive deck, level with house floor and supported by concrete columns (visible in photo at bottom of page) was built. Continuation of this deck around end of living room creates secluded sunbathing areas outside bedroom and study. Japanese lanterns, prints and sculpture were acquired by owner during stay in Japan

Morley Baer

Rental unit has every bit as much privacy as owners' part of house. Entrance (left) is on opposite side of garage, with similar approach from street via court and covered walk. Unit has two inner courts, one off dining area (above) which is currently used as a child's play space and one off living room. Bedrooms (not shown) overlook the creek at rear of property

Brentwood Garden Apartments

Los Angeles, Calif.

Dᴇsɪɢɴᴇᴅ ᴘʀɪᴍᴀʀɪʟʏ to simplify housekeeping problems for single people, these small apartments also offer a degree of comfort and privacy not often found in more stereotyped conceptions of "efficiency" units. The solution closely resembles a series of tiny row-houses, each with provision for outdoor living and individual front and rear entrances. To assure a garden-like quality, a generous budget was allowed for good plant material to carry out the landscape design of Evans and Reeves.

To the northeast, the irregular shaped lot is backed by a wooded canyon adjoining a government-owned Veterans' Hospital, and affords an open view of rolling hills. To take full advantage of this, and to give greater privacy, a staggered plan was developed with all living areas facing the view. Baths and kitchens on the south are shielded from an adjacent undeveloped lot, by plants and acacia trees flanking the entrance walk. A redwood grill is used to set off the entry to each unit, and to screen it from the neighboring apartments. Jointly-used service facilities and a special parking area for guests' cars are grouped at the front of the lot to form a buffer between living quarters and street traffic noises. Three of the apartments were planned for single occupancy. The fourth is a double unit with separate bedroom and study alcove.

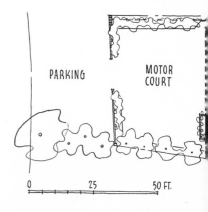

152 BRENTWOOD

APARTMENTS DESIGNED FOR SINGLE PEOPLE

Robert C. Cleveland Photos

Chalfant Head

Architect and Owner

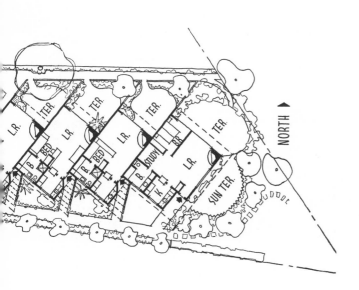

Robert C. Cleveland Photos

The repetitive patterns of set-backs and sloping roofs serve as both functional and design elements (above). Insulated blank wall at lower side of each unit shuts out intense summer heat on west exposure, gives greater sense of seclusion to garden. Shed roof permits clerestory to southeast for light and ventilation

Each of the compact single apartments offers complete facilities for comfortable living, has built-in storage to minimize furniture requirements. Left: glazed wall opens all-purpose room to patio Above: free-standing wardrobe separates sleeping and serving areas

Color and texture play an important part in the design of the frame structure. The rough redwood siding is trimmed in yellow for a warm contrast, and possible severity of the street facade was overcome by painting the interior of the open carport blue green. The entrance paths, and the main terrace of the double unit (right), are brick set in sand; the side terrace is gravel with staggered redwood edge. The patios of the single units are paved with red colored concrete to harmonize with alternating concave and convex panels of redwood fences

Robert C. Cleveland Photos

Double apartment includes same facilities as single units, plus bedroom and sleeping alcove (right). Alcove can be provided with folding door if desired Kitchen, seen through swinging door and pass window (above), is fitted, as are the other apartments, with prefabricated unit, has additional storage cabinet. Plastic-top dining counter in pass window doubles as bar for entertaining. All apartments are soundproofed with rockwool woven between studding. Heating is by floor slab radiant hot water system, with gas-fired boiler

Ceilings of all units are pale yellow for reflective light, floors are gray
asphalt tile to minimize upkeep. Fireplace hood is stamped aluminum

GOOD ARCHITECTURE PAYS DIVIDENDS

Bel Air Garden Apartments, West Los Angeles, Calif.

A. Quincy Jones, Jr., Architect

Edgardo Contini, Structural Engineer

Dickason Construction Co., Contractor

Julius Shulman Photos

Even such imponderables as a hilly site and mild climate are turned into revenue producing assets in this nine-unit apartment house. Sunny open air terraces (at right in photo below), balconies (right), and a central court (left) afford outdoor living areas, increase sense of spaciousness. Judicious use of screens gives privacy, permits occasional vistas

THAT CAREFUL ARCHITECTURAL PLANNING PAYS DIVIDENDS is evident in this California apartment house: after a year's occupancy, the project shows a 20 per cent of gross investment return, contrasted with 12 per cent usually expected.

The owners desired to build a "luxury" apartment house on a relatively small, expensive site. After analyzing costs of property, construction and improvements, it was determined that six one-bedroom and three two-bedroom units were required to insure a safe investment. To justify the high rent, the architect was faced with the problem of providing a sense of space, a garage, and at least a minimum private outdoor living area for each unit.

The final solution incorporates many amenities for pleasant living within the confines of the limited plot. The building centers around a common garden, which serves as entrance lobby and as space for entertaining large groups. In addition, each unit has a small terrace, screened by a 6-ft fence for privacy. All landscaping for the project was designed by the architect.

FIRST FLOOR

0 5 10 15 20 25 FT.

Julius Shulman Photos

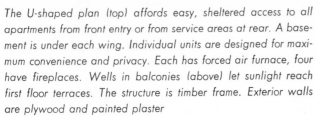

The U-shaped plan (top) affords easy, sheltered access to all apartments from front entry or from service areas at rear. A basement is under each wing. Individual units are designed for maximum convenience and privacy. Each has forced air furnace, four have fireplaces. Wells in balconies (above) let sunlight reach first floor terraces. The structure is timber frame. Exterior walls are plywood and painted plaster

BALCONY · CL · BEDRM · LAUN · K · LIVING RM · BEDRM

BEDRM · K · LIVING RM · B · CL · LIN · B

CL · CL · LIVING RM · BALCONY · Well · BEDRM · CL · LIN · B

LIVING RM · K. · CL · CL · BEDRM · BEDRM · CL · BEDRM

B · LIVING RM · K · CL · BEDRM · B · B · LIN · LIN · B

DECK · DECK · BEDRM · CL CL · BEDRM

Dn · Dn · Dn · Dn

SECOND FLOOR

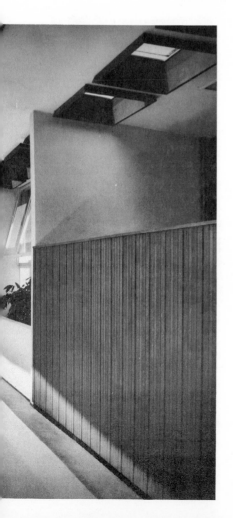

Wooden screens, integrated with building design (left), shield apartment entrances and extend usable living space (above). Openings in overhangs filter sunlight into living rooms

Pass windows and broad counters, as in this typical apartment (right and below), facilitate meal serving. Kitchen cabinets are finished in wood, walls are tile. Each apartment is equipped with refrigerator and built-in range and oven

Julius Shulman Photos

Service entrances and a garage for each apartment are located off the alley (right). The building has one laundry that can be scheduled for use. Each tenant is allotted 50 sq ft of storage area in the basement. The owner provides garden maintenance and limited maid service, and will also furnish an apartment if desired. Tenant reaction to the building and its operation is very favorable

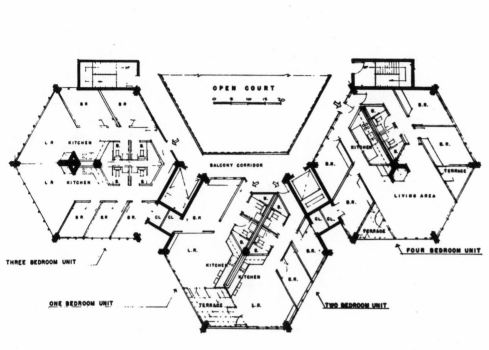

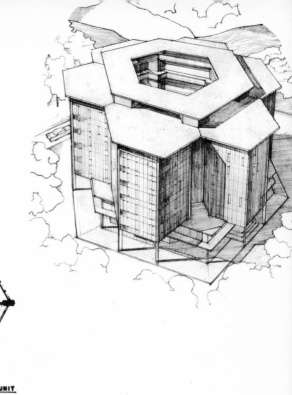

OPEN COURT

BALCONY CORRIDOR

THREE BEDROOM UNIT

ONE BEDROOM UNIT

FOUR BEDROOM UNIT

TWO BEDROOM UNIT

UNIQUE HOUSING IN THE OZARKS

*Cooperative Hunting Lodge
In The Ozark Mountains*

*Erhart, Eichenbaum, Rauch and Blass
Architects*

Situated on a long point of virgin forest land ending in a lake, this unique cooperative lodge is designed for a typical 20th century business need—expense account entertaining. The area boasts superb fishing and hunting; the site will be developed with boat docks, swimming areas, and a small golf course, with servants' quarters and garage nearby.

The open ground floor will house office and service only; the second floor club rooms and manager's suite; above, the hexagonal apartment units will be sold either as units or half-units. The plan suggests the variety of divisions possible for these.

The structural frame will be of concrete; the window wall of redwood and copper; air conditioning and heating units at each floor will be natural gas powered.

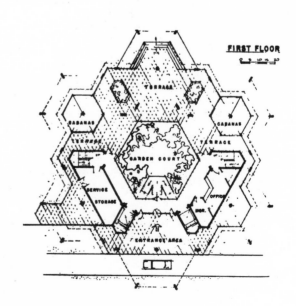

FIRST FLOOR

Julius Shulman Photos

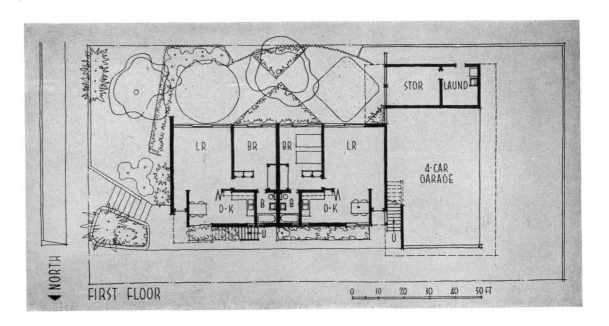

STOR   LAUND

LR   BR   BR   LR

4-CAR
GARAGE

D·K   D·K

NORTH

FIRST FLOOR

0   10   20   30   40   50 FT

315 SOUTH VIRGIL AVENUE, LOS ANGELES

Carl Louis Matson, Architect

Eckbo, Royston and Williams, Landscape Architects

THIS SIX-FAMILY APARTMENT HOUSE was built on a 60 by 120 ft lot in an old residential section only five minutes from the center of the city. The architect selected the property with the belief that many people would like to live close to their work and also enjoy some of the pleasures of outdoor living. His judgement proved correct and the apartments have been very popular, especially with young professional people.

Construction is of wood frame on concrete slab.

The area of the building proper is 3925 sq ft, plus 900 sq ft in laundry, storage, and carport. Built under separate contracts, the total cost was $32,000, including landscaping, carpets, draperies, ranges, refrigerators and garbage disposal units.

Sound insulation between floors is provided by resilient clips for ceiling lath and ½-in. fiberboard above the subflooring. Party walls employ staggered studs with continuous mineral wool blanket.

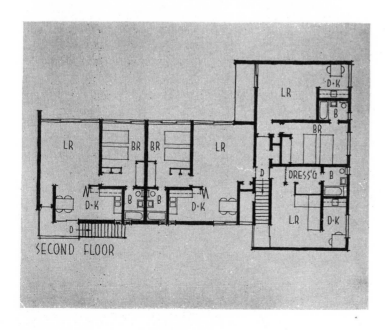

SECOND FLOOR

Of the six apartments four face south and all have through ventilation. Two apartments have balconies and two have terraces. Fences of corrugated asbestos-cement provide privacy for the attractively landscaped terraces. Sliding glass doors give access to balconies and terraces

Below: Folding partition may be used to separate kitchen from dining or to cut both off from the living room. Partition is made of mahogany plywood and moves on casters

FRANKLIN APARTMENTS, INC., ST. ALBANS, VT.

Whittier and Goodrich, Architects

GARDEN APARTMENTS all over the country are being forced to wear ill-fitting clothes copied from old New England houses. This straightforward design from Vermont may surprise some people, who had forgotten that New England is also famous for practicality and intellectual honesty.

This 20-family apartment building is of frame construction and was designed on a 4-ft module. End walls are solid brick. Side walls are brick veneer up to the first floor window sills and striated plywood above that level. Windows are steel casements with steel interior trim.

Apartments have from one to three bedrooms and are arranged two per stair per floor. A sloping site permits four apartments in the basement. The rest of the basement is used for laundry and drying rooms, storage lockers, and boiler room. All apartments have through ventilation, interior baths, and open kitchens.

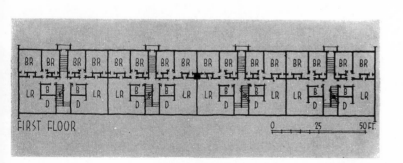

FIRST FLOOR   0   25   50 FT.

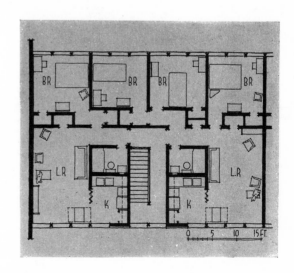

167

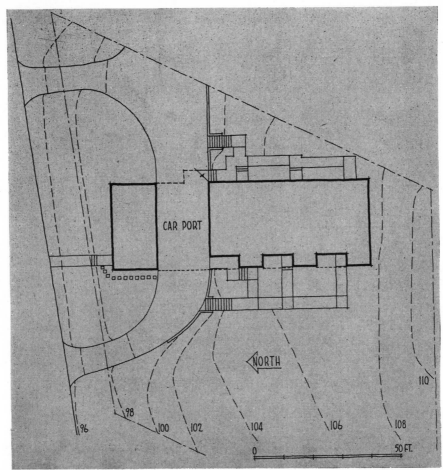

CAR PORT

NORTH

96 98 100 102 104 106 108 110

0 50 FT.

FIVE-FAMILY APARTMENT HOUSE

Jackson, Mississippi

James T. Canizaro, Architect and Engineer

THIS FIVE-FAMILY APARTMENT HOUSE is owned by the architect, who had little difficulty in convincing the owner of the soundness of his solution. The project was conventionally financed and the approval of FHA was not required.

The architect's solution to the problem presented by the irregular, steeply sloping site was to step a long thin building up the slope. The building contains four apartments with two bedrooms and one with one bedroom. The upper apartments are duplex suites with their bedrooms on the floor above. The result is that although there are three floors, no one has to walk more than one flight to reach his living room.

The two-bedroom apartments have a gross area of about 1000 sq ft. All apartments have through ventilation. The architect was able to retain some fine oaks on the upper level which provide summer shade for a large part of the building. Roof overhangs supplement the shade of the trees. Screened balconies are a pleasant feature of the duplex suites and for the greater part of the year their area can be added to the bedrooms. The balconies also provide protections for the main entrance and the living room windows on the floor below.

The building cost $42,900 including blinds, ranges, and refrigerators. The area of the building is approximately 4600 sq ft.

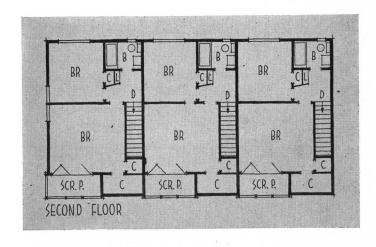

Below, left: first floor plan. Between, right: second floor; three units at right are duplexes. Above: third floor, upper level of duplex apartments. In the basement off carport are storage, servants' dressing room and lavatory

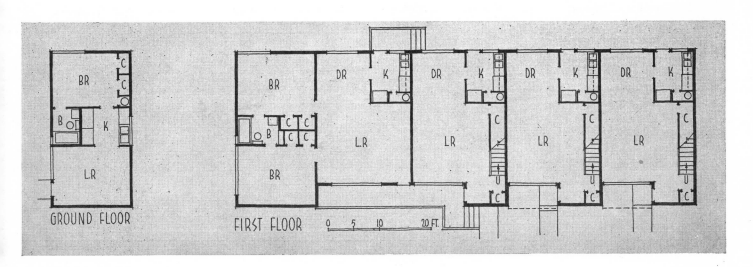

169

Frank Lotz Miller

NEW ORLEANS: RENTAL FLEXIBILITY AND PATIOS

The Patios Apartment, New Orleans

Curtis and Davis, Architects

Two interesting features characterize this two-story, 15-unit apartment. There is an unusual three-dimensional concept providing a private patio for each apartment, the second floor opening in, the ground floor opening out. And, rental flexibility is provided by an alternate plan in which two small efficiency apartments — each consisting of living-dining space, kitchen, bath and subdivided sleeping space — can be combined into a suite comprising living-dining space, study or guest room, kitchen, storage, two bedrooms and two baths. As actually built, all the apartments are small units except two, but the provision for possible future change is built-in.

Located on the edge of a high class residential neighborhood, the site is bounded on three sides by streets, on the fourth by houses, and was described by the architects as "very tight." Since few small apartments are available in the area and the demand for them is brisk, this project was aimed at the "luxury-efficiency" rental market, consisting of either young childless or older retired couples of middle income or above. Although not showily expensive, the use of such materials

as cork floors, mahogany panelling and acoustic ceilings places the building in the medium or slightly above rental scale. It has been solidly leased at planned rates since completion, yielding the owner a good profit.

The structure was limited to two stories in order to utilize light construction and avoid the requirement of elevators. Economies were effected by duplication of framing, use of standard lumber lengths, and by repetition of standard details, e. g., similar window-wall units assembled in the mill and simply secured in place on the job. The second floor patios are enclosed by corrugated plastic panels which are pleasantly translucent, economical, and easily supported on the light steel frame. Air conditioning was justified only on the basis of individual units, operated or not at the tenant's discretion. In actuality, they are nearly all in use constantly.

The building cost was slightly less than $12 per sq ft late in 1952. Maintenance has been very inexpensive, probably due to the natural wood interiors and to an exterior of cedar shakes, brick, natural wood fencing and plastic panels.

PATIO · B.R. · B. · B. · B.R. · B.R. · B. · B.R. · PARKING
K. · K. · PARKING
L. a D. · L. a D. · L. a D. · UT. · LAUN.

L. a D. · L. a D. · L. a D. · L. a D.
K. · K. · K. · K.
B.R. · B.R. · B.R. · B.R.
B. · B. · B. · B.
PATIO

GROUND FLOOR

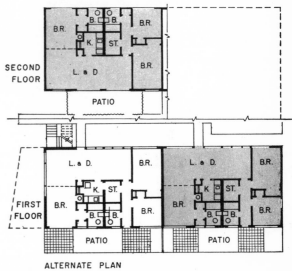

B.R. · B. · B. · B.R. · B.R. · B. · B.R. · B.R.
K. · K. · K. · B.
L. a D. · L. a D. · L. a D. · K.
PATIO · PATIO · PATIO · PATIO · L. a D.

PATIO · PATIO · PATIO · PATIO
L. a D. · L. a D. · L. a D. · K.
K. · K. · K. · B.
B.R. · B.R. · B.R. · B.R. · B.R.
B. · B.

SECOND FLOOR

0 5 10 20

B.R. · B. · B. · B.R.
K. · ST.
L. a D. · B.R.

SECOND
FLOOR

PATIO

L. a D. · B.R. · L. a D. · B.R.
K. · ST. · K. · ST.
B.R. · B.R.
B. · B. · B. · B.
B.R. · B.R.

FIRST
FLOOR

PATIO · PATIO

ALTERNATE PLAN

The alternate plan, directly above, shows the manner in which two small apartments can readily be converted to a larger suite. At left, entrance from street; bottom left, view of the second floor corridor looking into a private patio; bottom right, typical apartment living area — note natural wood wall finishes

Hedrich-Blessing

CHICAGO: WIDE VARIETY OF APARTMENT SIZES

The Pioneer Cooperative, Inc.

CONCEIVED in an effort to provide better housing at reasonable cost in Chicago's Hyde Park area, near the University of Chicago, this project has proved successful in reaching that goal and in two other respects as well: first, as an example of good apartment house design; and second, in acting as a key factor for the coming redevelopment of an old neighborhood sliding downhill.

With the help of architect and builder, the venture was started by a like-minded group, each owner holding shares in proportion to the size of his apartment. Costs were held to a minimum; there were no promotion fees in the early budget. Although a wide variety of apartment sizes was required, no particular number was specified, the idea being to keep land cost per unit in line with reasonable rentals in a non-profit setup. Study of all factors resulted in a scheme housing 23 families in units ranging from one bedroom suites to 6-room row houses. A typical tenant-owner in a 4-room apartment, for example, made a down payment of $5470 and pays a $95 fixed monthly charge, which entitles him to a tax deduction of roughly $380. The fixed charge covers amortization, taxes, insurance, maintenance and required reserve. Individuals pay for electricity; do their own decorating. As rents rise, the owner-occupants' relative advantage becomes more apparent daily.

The neighborhood is an old one containing pockets of blight and is practically 100 per cent built-up. However,

this particular plot was vacant, tax delinquent, easy to acquire and is convenient to public transport, the University of Chicago, an elementary school and a shopping center. In spite of these favorable factors, private financing sources shied away from the generally deteriorating character of the area so that financing had to be arranged through FHA. This caused changes, which, according to the architects' estimates, probably increased cost as much as 10 per cent. However, the project was completed for $268,000 or $1.15 per cu ft exclusive of land cost and the architects' fee.

The architects' hope that rebuilding would help reverse the downward trend of the neighborhood has been reinforced by the recent start of a master plan for the area's redevelopment by the University of Chicago together with two neighborhood groups under a Field Foundation grant. The Pioneer project will form an important key in such a scheme.

The two-building, L-shaped arrangement (see plans) covers 32 per cent of the land, provides paved off-street parking for 60 per cent of the tenants, orients to a garden area, and provides both indoor and outdoor play space for the children. The fireproof structures are supported on a combination concrete frame and brick bearing wall system; the floor slabs contain hot water heating coils; sub-partitions are 2-in. solid plaster; finish floors are asphalt tile; ceilings are painted exposed concrete.

George Fred Keck —
William Keck,
Architects

Robert Bruce Tague,
Associate Architect

Frank Kornacker & Associates,
Structural Engineers.

William Goodman,
Heating Engineer

Perry Construction Company,
Builders

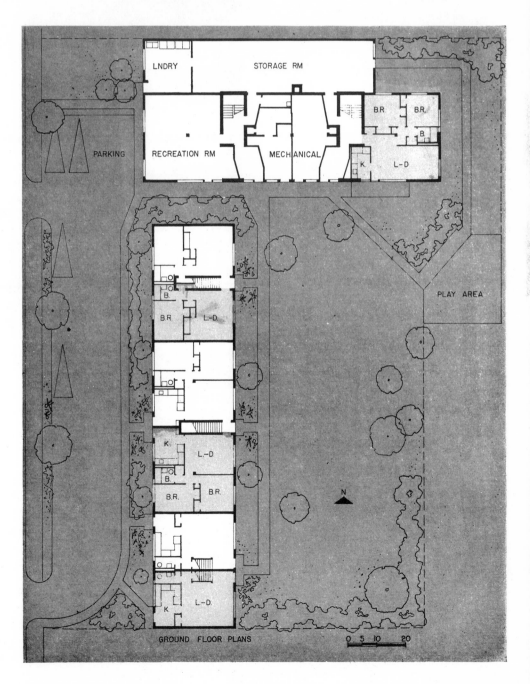

GROUND FLOOR PLANS   0 5 10 20

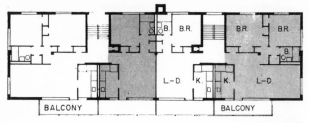

TYPICAL UPPER FLOOR

SECOND FLOOR

The upper photo shows the projecting balconies on the north building. which shade the large glass areas in summer but permit the sun to penetrate inside in winter, and provide private outdoor space for each apartment. The railings are of typical chain link fencing, supported on galvanized standard structural sections. The lower photo looks out over a typical apartment balcony.

Hedrich-Blessing

V Campus
Dormitories and Apartments

DORMITORY DESIGN:
ECONOMICAL HOUSING ISN'T ENOUGH

By ALBERT BUSH-BROWN, *Assistant Professor, Architectural History, Massachusetts Institute of Technology*

PRIMARY among the facts to be faced by the architect of dormitories is the individual student himself. Outwardly perhaps no different from the boy who becomes a truck driver or mechanic, no different from the girl who marries or becomes a salesgirl, the student nonetheless is separated from these by different ambitions: he shunts aside temporarily — and sometimes forever — the accepted goods of financial return, domesticity and gregariousness. He arrives at college sensitive to values in uncommon areas of culture. For him, isolation, small-group housing, a chance to select what is compatible to his personality and objectives, are important. Students occupying hotel-like dormitories often discover to their pleasure that a room rented in a house is preferable to the small cell on a bleak corridor available at college. They find in the house a scale, a warmth, a compatibility of environment with personal values, and an intimate group of friends in harmony with their needs and ambition. If the architect ignores the scholar's needs for privacy, domestic scale and identification with a small environment, his dormitories will miss the mark.

The architect will also miss the mark if he fails to recognize the collective identity existing within groups of students and the educational benefits attendant upon such identity. Proximity to other students provokes greater concentration upon learning, but it also accentuates the uniqueness of men who sever customary ties with non-academic goals, loose the bonds of identity with small communities and lower schools, and develop loyalties to higher institutions, new friends and quests. This is a disruptive process, easier for some students than others, but it is not aided by the dormitory conceived entirely as a series of cellular bedroom-studies precluding any activities that make education a corporate experience. Nor is it necessarily aided by a multi-purpose room (that horrible admission of unclear planning!) in combination with dormitory cells. What is needed is a plan containing spaces of well-defined use capable of nurturing contact among students, encouraging common participation and endeavor in specific, objective activities that release student energies.

Besides providing spaces and scale ranging all the way from individually private to corporate, the architecture of a residential system must also recognize the variety existing among students. Some arrive self-disciplined, others ready to explore all facets of bohemianism, and still others are insecure, possibly from an unrecognized need for outer control. Some are gregarious, others mavericks, and still others constricted by shyness.

All this variety presents problems for the architect and educator seeking the common denominator. Should he plan to have men live singly, in pairs, in suites, in rooms all alike? Should he provide rooms and apartments for faculty residents? Should he have long corridors with many small rooms, or suites opening off short stairwells? If, for reasons of expediency or financial economy, he is too ready to accept the minimum, standardized solution to dormitory planning, the architect may fail to obtain that variety and those controls needed by individual students, while planning for a fictionalized statistic who does not exist.

Moreover the architect must face the realities of student habits. Not all activities enjoyed by students are civilized or meditative or scholarly. They are not encompassed by studying, eating, sleeping and relaxing. What about the light controls needed by a student who still must test the long-proven false notion that man works best throughout the night? What acoustical treatment is required to protect others from the background music or the typewriter working against tomorrow morning's deadline? What materials will resist the scars of baseball played indoors? The function of a room is hardly defined by the name an architect gives it, but rather by the limits of a student's imagination. There he may rehearse a play, meet with others to speak French, discuss religion, play bridge; there he may first follow a Beethoven symphony in the score, assemble his personal library, propose to his future wife. But just as likely he may become intent upon reassembling a stripped-down Ford within the fourth floor shower room.

The architect can not, of course, plan for any of these activities, but the personality of his dormitory has got to suggest the range and warmth they imply. There is little an architect can do about the annual Spring riot, which is as predictable as the coming of final examinations; an architect can not prevent it, but the plan and materials he selects may well control that riot or at least save the university some maintenance bills.

Should a University Supply Dormitories?

Opinion is still divided today, as it has been since the fourteenth century, on the question of how best to serve the needs of this special client, the student. There are still those who believe that the university should offer only intellectual education, permitting students to live in fraternities, apartments, rented rooms or wherever they may wish. There are others who believe equally strongly that a college or university is responsible for the total training of an individual, including social and personal education, and must provide a residential system. Traditionally, the first point of view has been held by educators at universities, the latter by teachers at colleges.

Because of the complexity of individuals they house and the range of conditions they must meet, systems of residence have not always been successful. Dormitories built by colleges in the eighteenth and early nineteenth century were especially inadequate as regards crowding, ventilation, illumination, heating, dampness, noise, fire-protection and furnishings.

No dormitories were built at M.I.T. or the Johns Hopkins, and while Cornell was forced by its rural location to provide residences, Harvard saw no additional dormitories built for undergraduates during a large period of Eliot's long presidency between 1871 and 1909.

This important detour from the older English collegiate practice was made at universities where educators emulated German and other continental universities. In Germany, universities provided only lecture halls, libraries, laboratories and a main hall suitable for holding ceremonies. Students attending a German university obtained their own lodging and board. Such was the respect for the product graduated by German universities that many educators in America attempted to introduce university organization by either beginning new institutions such as the Johns Hopkins or superimposing university structure upon the colleges, as was done at Harvard. Many remnants of the system are still visible, particularly at urban universities, such as New York University, and graduate schools, such as that at Michigan, as well as in technological institutes,

such as M.I.T., which has not yet fully converted to the residential system for undergraduates.

Aligned against all their arguments are those educators who believe that higher education should continue the English collegiate tradition of being concerned with educating the whole man. They conceive that the primary objective of the residential system is to assist the institution in providing a better educational program; housing students is a secondary aim. American history is full of eminent men who supported this belief: all the early college educators, Jefferson, McCosh, Porter, Abbot Lawrence Lowell who developed the brilliant scheme for the Houses at Harvard, Woodrow Wilson and Andrew Fleming West who together helped shape the residential pattern at Princeton, and Compton and Killian who were instrumental in modifying the pattern for use at M.I.T.

Their belief in the educational effectiveness of a good residential system rests on one fact: intellectual life at those institutions possessing good residential systems is more vigorous than at those institutions where they are lacking. List the top institutions in the country on the basis of educational worth; each has physical accommodations that promote active common life. In some cases, the residential system may be supplemented by a favorable residential neighborhood, or by fraternities, but the heart of the common life lies in the residential system.

To sum up, there are five major reasons for supporting the idea of having good residential systems:

1. *The absence of a residential system may be one factor in lowering academic performance.* A striking instance of this occurred at a university in a large Middle Western city which had for a long time enjoyed high academic attainment by students who resided in houses near the campus. In the period around 1918 when good rooms were still available in private houses in the neighborhood, the absence of a dormitory system was not serious. But when, after the depression, the neighborhood became increasingly less residential, the university could no longer easily attract young men and especially young women from areas lying outside the metropolitan limits.

"Student needs do not change substantially from generation to generation, and it is important therefore to build upon a plan that is enduring, whether the actual building is considered temporary or not. For this the excellent traditions at Oxford, where New College dormitories date from about 1400, are still worth studying."

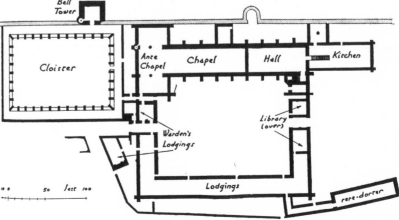

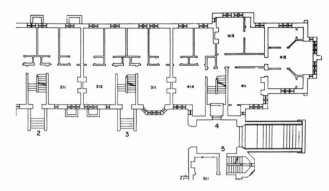

Cuyler Hall, Princeton University, a "good example of what may be done"

2. *Still another result of the absence of a good residential system is divisionism among students.* The dormitory is democratic, embracing everyone; its substitutes tend to separate people according to intellectual interest in studies, social position and friendships, economic advantage, religion or race.

3. *Adequately planned residential systems foster life in common, with desirable educational effects.* All a student really learns he gets by the active operation of his own intellect. Here his environment, including his fellows and place of residence, are important. If he is overly specialized, as many students are, he needs contact with a community of interests. He needs to be provoked to think on many subjects, exchanging views, acquiring a corporate spirit of mutual inspiration, liberality of thought, breadth of view, and even some training in responsible citizenship.

4. *It also decreases emphasis upon certain other aspects of college life.* I like to think that the downfall of Harvard's early twentieth century preeminence in football — so greatly missed by Harvard graduates — is in some part due to the enormous success of the thoroughly praise-worthy house system, begun tentatively about 1929 and fully in operation now. That house system was largely developed by a great educator, Abbott Lawrence Lowell, and it was he who, to my knowledge, first revealed that the increasing emphasis on mass spectator sports — so well emphasized by the building of the huge Harvard stadium shortly after the turn of the century — was due in large measure to the fact that they then provided the only means for displaying the corporate spirit of the institution. Lacking any common life in the elective system of education and residence, the undergraduate found in the football spectacle his major evidence of institutional solidarity.

5. *The residential system which encourages a common, institutional life may realize some incidental financial benefits.* It builds identifications with institutions that result in alumni loyalty. Clark University at Worcester is often cited as an instance of a non-residential university, which failed to enlist the financial support of alumni in retaining its former eminence.

Planning the Residential System

At a minimal level, much can be accomplished by having a series of separate dormitories, in combination with a student union or dining hall for general use. This plan was adapted at many older universities such as Harvard, where, shortly after the Civil War, Memorial Hall served as dining hall for students housed in many separate dormitories and private residences. Where the institution is large, the disadvantages of this system are obvious.

Within dormitories, architects may adopt several types of circulation. Standards are the corridors, either single or double loaded, served by either staircases or elevators. These have the usual advantages.

A plan not used recently but of the oldest merit should be recalled, the multiple-entry system. Traditional ways of using it seem to involve additional expense and to consume more ground area than is normally available; but this plan has not had the study it deserves. Among the advantages obtainable in the multi-entry system are these:

1. *reduction of corridor traffic;*

2. *division of the plan into small units capable of producing better scale, easier relation to irregular sites;*

3. *more privacy;*

4. *greater variety;*

5. *division of dormitory into smaller units thereby encouraging identification with entry and greater responsibility for protecting and caring for property;*

6. *protection against mass assembly and riots;*

7. *better light and acoustical insulation;*

8. *reduction of structural bays;*

9. *improved fire protection.*

There are some disadvantages in the need for additional staircases, particularly where a second means of egress is required, but the plan needs to be studied further by modern architects. Particularly happy older applications exist in dormitories at Harvard, Princeton, Haverford, Yale and Trinity College.

Rooms within dormitories have tended recently to be bedroom-studies, all alike, intended either for single or double occupancy. It is questionable in many cases whether equal space might not be arranged in a series of suites consisting of common living room-studies with as many as four private or double bedrooms nearby. The houses at Harvard and the Pyne Dormitory and Cuyler Hall at Princeton offer good examples of what may be done.

Above all architects must realize that dormitories

Walter R. Fleischer

Dunster House, Harvard University

are less subject to obsolescence than many other types of building. Massachusetts Hall at Harvard is still in partial use as a dormitory, though it was built in 1718. Student needs do not change substantially from generation to generation, and it is important therefore to build upon a plan that is enduring, whether the actual building is considered temporary or not. For this the excellent traditions at Oxford, where New College dormitories date from about 1400, are still worth studying.

There are, however, some modern needs generally inadequately provided for in dormitories. Some institutions run summer schools and conferences, and for them air conditioned dormitories may be useful. Transportation facilities are often overlooked, particularly provisions for bicycles and automobiles. Curiously some architects have forgotten that books and their storage are major items in student rooms. Recently, students have found increasingly useful an area fitted as a laundry and another where kitchen facilities are available. There are other service machines that students attract: particularly hard to place unless specific provisions have been made are the various dispensaries of coke, candy and cigarettes which clutter too many hallways. Contact with home and the town is important, and adequate provisions should be made for telephones and mail delivery. Also in the perimeter of the dormitory students need some kind of private area, well landscaped, where the Spring pastime of sunbathing can be conducted with less disturbance to the general aspect of the campus.

But more important than the dormitories alone is the residential system as a whole where dormitories are combined with adequate dining rooms, libraries, common rooms and sports areas. The best of the systems so arranged are to be found in the Houses at Harvard, which are based upon the colleges at Oxford and Cambridge. Approximations of the system exist at Yale, and other institutions; notably California at Berkeley, M.I.T.; and many women's colleges have similar systems. The basic idea contained therein is to form a complete, self-sustaining residential complex. Several dormitory wings are arranged around courts from which multiple entries open. Within the dormitories are suites for students, residences for tutors, a master and his family and studies for non-resident faculty members. Nearby are kitchens, dining halls, libraries, a common room with magazines and exhibits of painting, and game rooms. Frequently, as at Adams House at Harvard, old buildings are easily incorporated into the new houses.

Even in the house system, with all its advantages to education, there have been many recent concessions to lower standards of living, and it's generally conceded that the new house, soon to be erected at Harvard, will not provide the degree of elegance obtained twenty-five years ago when Lowell and Eliot Houses were built, or the Graduate College at Princeton.

Three-fold Purpose

Many educators today recognize a three-fold purpose in higher education; to lead young people in attaining competence in intellectual affairs; to develop personal character and social responsibility; and to aid in forming patterns of behavior, thought and imagination which will best foster living happily and generously. Towards these ends the formal curriculum and its methods of education by means of lectures, seminars, conferences, research and theses, contribute. But common life, especially in the residential system, is regarded as playing an enormous role.

The architect's plan for a dormitory must, in the long run, help the university to teach self-respect and respect for the rights, beliefs and habits of other men; it must help to enlarge the capacity to understand strange and opposing points of view, customs and preferences; and to foster in students the kinds of decorum expected in the manners, dress and speech of educated men.

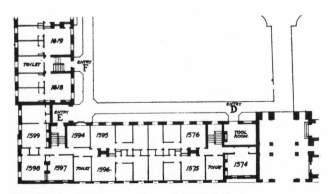

Timothy Dwight College, Yale University, one of the "house" system dormitories with many entries and small student groups

179

MEN'S DORMITORY WITH SOCIAL ROOMS

DORMITORY HOUSES 114 men, mostly in double rooms. There are six living-study rooms, one for every 17 to 20 students. Corridors are narrow (3 ft 6 in.) with recesses serving four rooms each in order to cut down apparent length of corridor and assist somewhat in acoustical problems. Typical bedroom has built-in closets and bureaus, book shelf and desks. On the ground floor there are commons rooms which are to serve other students besides those in this building, the campus needing more social space: a large lounge with separate parlors, table tennis room and kitchenette. Outdoor space on adjacent terrace will considerably extend the social areas in seasonable weather. Storage space is exceptionally large, as students are in school six months, away working the other six. *Corry Hall, Antioch College, Yellow Springs, Ohio. Skidmore, Owings & Merrill, Architects.*

Hedrich-Blessing

Technical Data: lift-slab, Youtz-Slick system. Square columns built up of two 8-by-8-in. steel angles filled with concrete. Exterior walls, salmon colored brick with lightweight concrete block backup, furred and plastered. Windows in bedrooms are double hung aluminum, with precast concrete spandrel below. Edges of concrete floor and roof slabs are exposed flush with face of brick in-filled panels.

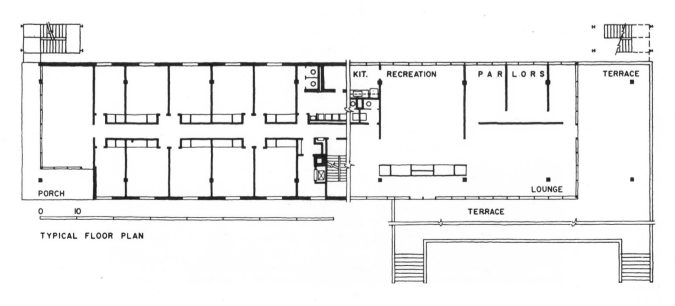

TYPICAL FLOOR PLAN

KIT. RECREATION PARLORS TERRACE

PORCH

LOUNGE

TERRACE

0   10

DORMITORIES WITH CLASSROOMS

To MEET an urgent need for on-campus living quarters and classrooms Rutgers has combined the two in three new buildings. The group also includes a student lounge building, which is calculated to focus social life in this new section of the campus. "The architects and the University," say the architects, "approached the many problems of planning with the basic concept that today's student, no matter at what level, is a social being and that he functions best, academically, physically and socially, when he feels at home." The site, a narrow, steeply sloping strip along the Raritan River, made it possible to keep classroom and dormitory circulation at different levels. *Dormitory and Classroom Group, Rutgers University, New Brunswick, N. J. Kelly & Gruzen, Architects; Martin L. Beck, associate in charge.*

Copyright 1957 by F. W. Dodge Corporation

Technical Data: Construction is fire-proofed steel frame, concrete floors, with cavity-type exterior walls, with brick colors to complement those of other campus buildings. Cost of the buildings: $4,000,000. Weiskopf & Pickworth, Structural Engineers; Mongitore & Moesel, Mechanical Engineers; Clarke & Rapuano, Landscape Architects.

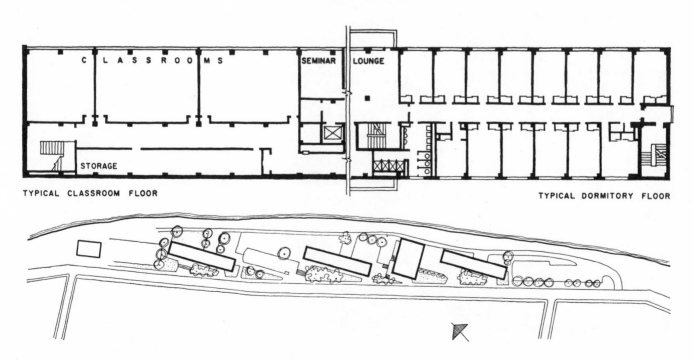

TYPICAL CLASSROOM FLOOR

TYPICAL DORMITORY FLOOR

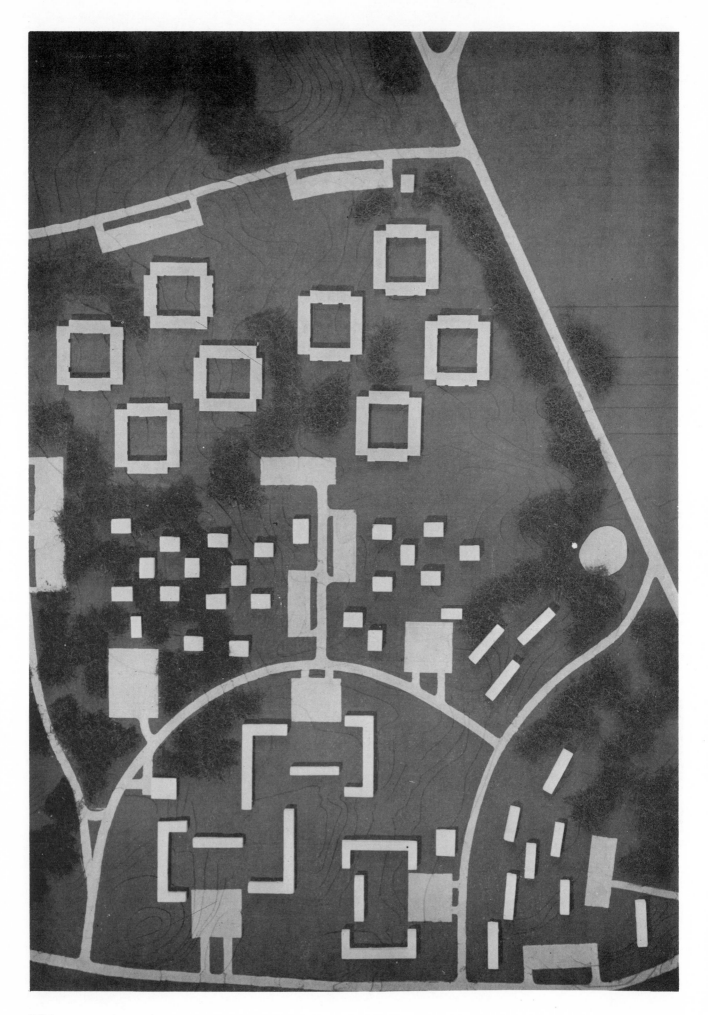

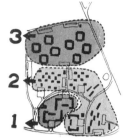

Hedrich-Blessing

CAMPUS HOUSING IN NEW AND VARIED PATTERNS

Northwood Apartment Group, University of Michigan, Ann Arbor, Mich.

Yamasaki, Leinweber and Associates, Architects and Engineers

As ARCHITECTS work always toward more human values in housing developments, particularly when designing large groups, they push always farther into the realm of innovative ideas or find new combinations of old ideas. The site plan photograph on the opposite page shows schematic variations these architects have used for a large group of housing units for the University of Michigan. Though there are other efforts not visible in the site plan, it is still clear that the different types of buildings indicated will obviate the institutional atmosphere of "public housing" which could easily have crept into so large a project.

The architects explain that this is but a preliminary scheme — already there have been refinements of the third group of buildings indicated at the top of the photograph. As the small diagram shows, the project is being done in three groups, the third group still existing only on paper.

The first group was built on the highest, flattest part of a beautiful site with gently rolling contours. The architects, wanting to break with the more formal lines of the main campus, used the U and L type buildings to delineate informal and varied courts. The pattern changes in the second group, using a compact rowhouse scheme; the buildings are also informally placed, as dictated by the natural contours of the land. There is still another pattern within this group; four small apartment units are placed back to back on each floor of compact rectangular buildings. This design is economical since porches are eliminated.

The third group, as now proposed, uses a slightly more formal, enclosed court; this scheme would use quite similar plans but would give the buildings a different character. The separate buildings are disposed in a thoroughly informal pattern.

Various differences in design and materials also contribute to a visual change of pace. The architects have chosen different shades of the same type of brick for the several types of buildings.

185

Hedrich-Blessing

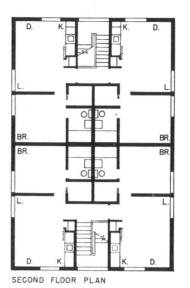

SECOND FLOOR PLAN

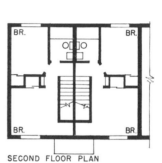

SECOND FLOOR PLAN

FIRST FLOOR PLAN

A beautiful site with gentle contours and large trees, which were saved, contributed heavily toward the final environment that the architects sought. Open sections for entrances and stairs break up the rows of apartments and provide a see-through openness, not to mention covered porches beside each apartment. Plans are various combinations of row houses, and one-bedroom units

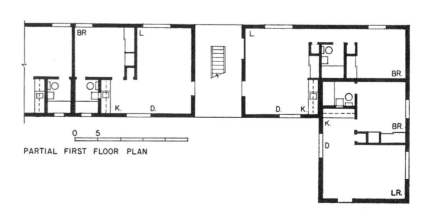

PARTIAL FIRST FLOOR PLAN

0 5

187

Interiors generally manage a simple and informal elegance and a feeling of openness. Windows are arranged in large groups to provide a maximum of light and view but to give also plenty of wall space within for efficient furniture arrangement. Wherever possible the living-dining spaces are kept open right through the building. Exteriors were deliberately varied in fenestration as well as in brick colors, as part of the whole effort to avoid monotony

COLLEGE FACULTY HOUSING IN A

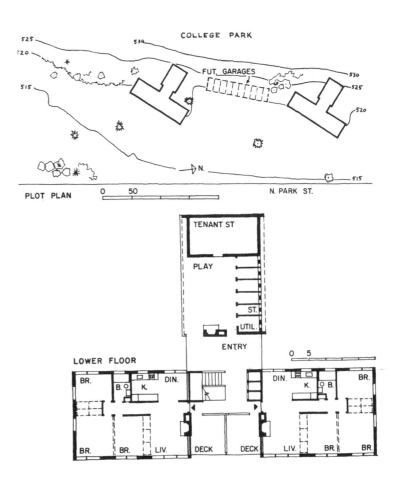

PLOT PLAN

COLLEGE PARK

FUT. GARAGES

N. PARK ST.

0   50

LOWER FLOOR

TENANT ST

PLAY

ST.

UTIL.

ENTRY

0   5

BR.   DIN.

B.   K.

BR.   BR.   LIV.   DECK

DIN.   K.   B.   BR.

DECK   LIV.   BR.   BR.

All photos by Joseph W. Molitor

Dartmouth Faculty Apartments,
Hanover, New Hampshire

E. H. & M. K. Hunter, Architects

Trumbull Nelson Company
General Contractors

In designing this attractive faculty housing for young members with growing families, the architects studied with particular care both the siting of the units and the specific needs of the tenants as individuals and as a group.

A nine-page questionnaire was distributed and several meetings were held to discuss the program; as a result, heavy emphasis was placed on children's play, storage of playthings, laundry facilities, noise isolation, and safe stairs.

WOODED SETTING

The site selected by the architects—after evaluating several—borders a college park, is convenient to classes, and is well situated for children's play. Based on a two-story maximum and a density of 5 families per acre, two buildings of 5 apartments each were located 170 ft apart and as far from the street as possible. The resulting wooded area around and between the structures provides privacy, sound insulation, and pleasant sylvan outlooks.

The plan features a central two-story entrance porch, serving as sound buffer and fire-break between apartments. At ground level, each building provides a protected play area with outdoor fireplace, flanked by individual storage cubicles for playthings.

The wood frame and brick buildings rise over grade-slabs. Since the convectors receive heat from the central college plant, basements could be eliminated.

Renderings by Jack Finnegan

SECOND FLOOR

FIRST FLOOR

UNIVERSITY HOUSING
BY EDWARD D. STONE

MARRIED STUDENTS APARTMENTS,   UNIV. OF ARKANSAS

This pleasant, orderly group of buildings gives a carefully studied solution to the problem of housing married students, which has developed since World War II. The design, done under a limited budget, places buildings around the site periphery, with social courts at the inner side (above), utility courts and parking toward the street. Screened and trellised terraces are at building intersections. The group will include 28 buildings (right); five are now nearing completion. Buildings are two-storied with ten apartments on each level. Structures are concrete block, reinforced concrete slabs. Each apartment has a living-dining area, kitchen alcove, porch, two bedrooms, bath. A stair serves each two units (left). The project was under the direction of University President Dr. John Caldwell.

Bob's of Fayetteville

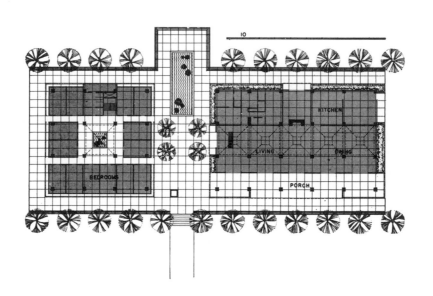

FRATERNITY HOUSE, UNIVERSITY OF ARKANSAS

Stone has developed a bi-nuclear scheme for this new house for the Alpha Gamma Rho Fraternity. The design separates the house according to function: a quiet bedroom-study wing, and a living-dining-entertainment wing. These are placed on a terrace platform overlooking the campus of the University of Arkansas, in Fayetteville. A covered walk will connect the wings. In the dormitory unit, rooms for 56 members are grouped around a two-story, skylighted lounge. A chapter room is in the basement. The living wing includes apartments for the house mother and the house manager, and a guest room. The interior of the main living space is roofed by five pyramidal skylights. A covered porch and the terrace expand entertainment space. A large portion of both wings will be "veiled" by concrete block grilles.

Louis Checkman

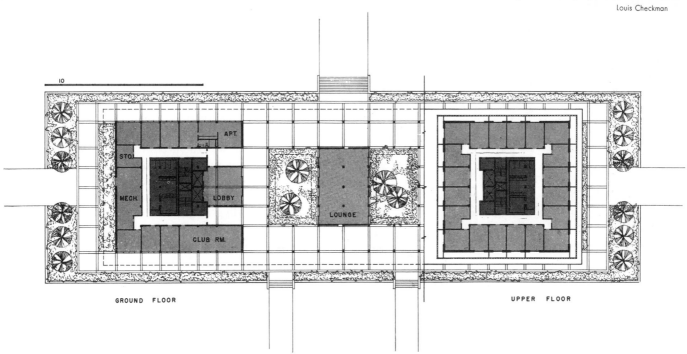

GROUND FLOOR   UPPER FLOOR

Russell B. Maxey

DORMITORIES, UNIVERSITY OF SOUTH CAROLINA

G. Thomas Harmon, Architect; Edward D. Stone, Associate Architect. Twin seven-story dormitory towers, linked by a common ground-level lounge and terrace make a simple, bold scheme for this men's residence hall in Columbia, South Carolina. These two, which are now under construction, are the first of a total of six to be built. On the grille exterior, Stone states, "Southern educators have complained of the glassy, contemporary style of dormitories, with the problem of heat, glare and privacy. The concrete veil overcomes these difficulties; its cost was about $1.00 per sq ft in place—about the price of venetian blinds per sq ft. The air conditioning load is reduced by about one third." The plan was developed under University President Russell. Landscape is by Innocenti & Webel.

195

NEW DORMITORIES AT CLEMSON COLLEGE

Site, structural system, budget and college customs determine design of dormitory quadrangle at Clemson, S. C.

CLEMSON'S NEW DORMITORIES, familiarly known as the "Barracks" and in use now since the fall of 1954, show in their design the positive influence of a number of easily identified factors. One is the site, which is restricted, was encumbered with inefficient old buildings (including some dormitories which it was cheaper to raze and replace than to remodel) and which drops off about 35 feet in its width.

Another factor was the necessity for speed; although some design preliminaries had been undertaken before the state appropriated construction funds (Clemson is a land-grant college), final design, working drawings and actual building all had to be compressed into less than two years. The architects determined upon lift-slab construction as the speediest construction system, with movable metal interior partitions, prefabricated

Architects: Lyles, Bissett, Carlisle & Wolff; G. H. Rowe, Structural Engineer; F. H. Franklin, Mechanical Engineer; Daniel Construction Co., General Contractors

cabinet walls between pairs of dormitory rooms, and exterior walls of steel sash members filled partly with windows, partly with insulated metal panels.

These structural decisions also met the requirements of the very strict budget, although a few items had to be cut out of the final design. For instance, air conditioning for the large Mess Hall which was an essential part of the group could not be installed under the original contract. However, ductwork, space for equipment. etc., was installed for a future air conditioning plant.

Since Clemson is a military school, military formations and drills had to be provided for. Halls in the dormitories are wide enough for this, the plaza which the buildings surround is a parade ground, and the entries into it through many of the buildings are in effect sally ports, wide enough for formations to pass through.

At the same time the group could not have a forbidding, fortress-like look. Originally it had been hoped that no unit would have to be more than four stories high. The number of students to be accommodated — 2000, in double rooms — made five stories necessary at some points. Certain characteristics of lift-slab construction and the slope of the site were turned to advantage in this connection. A single lift-slab console (control unit) can handle a 12-column lift; two together can handle 24 columns, and this determined the size of units into which the group is divided. The units step down across the slope, following the contours, and are separated by fire stairs. The fact that some units are set back from the others lessened the need for lateral

In an irregular U-plan, buildings surround a 2-level plaza used for military formations

bracing, reduced expansion problems, and has kept the parts of the group in human scale.

As one of the few five-story lift-slab jobs in the country, Clemson Barracks' construction posed some unusual problems. The columns, H-sections in bays 25 by 24 ft, would be too tall for their unbraced height if the top slab were lifted the full five stories at once. Instead, fourth and fifth floor slabs were lifted slightly above third floor level, on columns extending only that high, and were there anchored temporarily. Second and third floor slabs were then lifted and secured permanently, additional column sections were welded to the lower sections, and the top floor slabs were lifted to their final position.

Joseph W. Molitor

Central block in photo above is the College's Student Union; the low structure to its left is the Mess Hall, which can be reached without going outdoors — a necessity in inclement weather

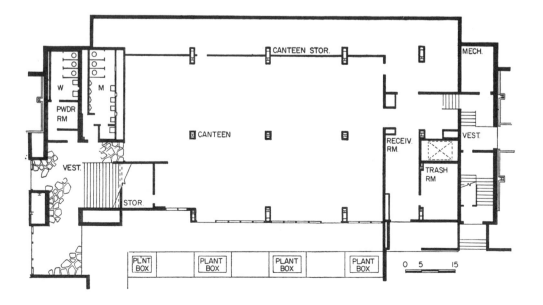

Below, canteen interior

MESS HALL LEVEL: Mess Hall and its kitchen facilities are designed to accommodate 3500 students, and for banquets, etc. To keep within the strict budget, air conditioning was omitted but ductwork, space, etc., were provided for future

Joseph W. Molitor

Central block of the group, originally offices and meeting rooms, has actually developed into the Student Union shown on these two pages. Section below shows how grade changes were utilized to provide entrances at several levels

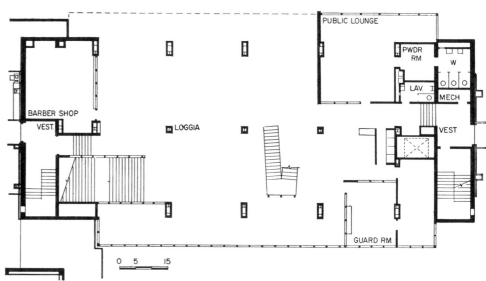

PUBLIC LOUNGE

PWDR RM

W

LAV.

MECH

BARBER SHOP

VEST.

LOGGIA

VEST

GUARD RM

0   5   15

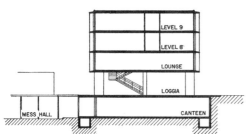

LEVEL 9

LEVEL 8

LOUNGE

LOGGIA

MESS HALL

CANTEEN

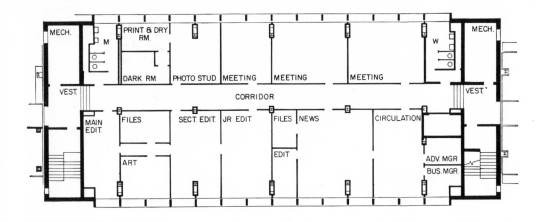

LEVEL 9: *While there are nine floor levels in all, at no place is the building more than five stories. Above, sketch of a meeting room as originally designed*

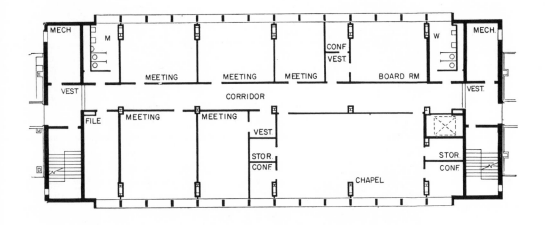

LEVEL 8: *Religious as well as social activities are provided for in the Student Union, as the photograph of the Chapel Altar, above, indicates*

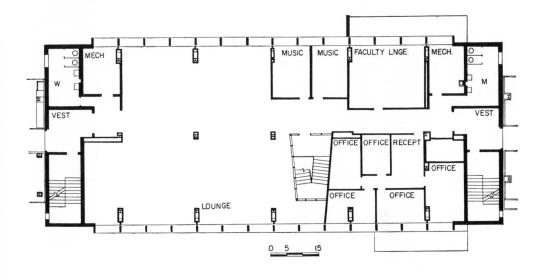

LEVEL 7: *Above is one of the lounges in the Student Union. Because a heavy floor load existed in this section, a "waffle" slab poured over plastic pans was used*

The design module, a dormitory room for two men, was studied carefully, even to making full-scale mock-ups. Rooms 12 ft. wide were chosen. Column bays 12 by 12 ft. were at first thought most economical, but 24-by-25-ft bays meant larger slab units, etc., and so were used. Partitions between pairs of rooms were initially cinder block; however, for a job this size the higher material cost of movable metal partitions was more than offset by their lower installation costs. Closet partitions were only slightly modified as design progressed; plumbing chase was carefully located for least interference with flat slab reinforcing. Exterior walls are curtains of steel sash members filled with either windows or insulated metal panels, with a continuous heating element at sill height

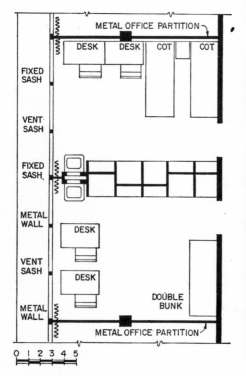

Quality
Accommodations

Ben Schnall

HOUSING BY BREUER

THE INSTITUTE FOR ADVANCED STUDY, PRINCETON, N. J.

For A Community
Of Distinguished
Scholars

Continental Air Views

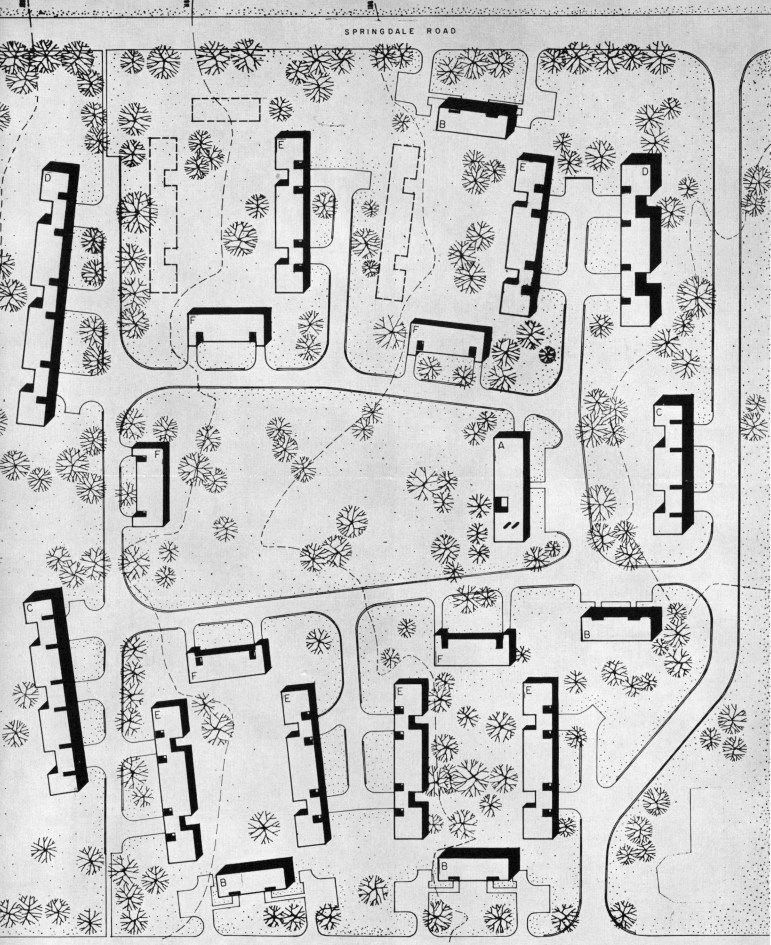

GOLF COURSE

N

SPRINGDALE ROAD

OLDEN LANE

INSTITUTE

0 50

The membership of the Institute For Advanced Study is composed of scholars selected for their attainments in mathematics, physics, or historical study. Their ages vary; some are unmarried; the majority have families. But all have in common an ardent devotion to the pursuit of learning, and all are situated in a semi-retreat away from the town. In designing housing for such a group, individual comforts and amenities were of course a basic requirement for the units and their siting. But the provision of an environment and facilities for the community spirit of the membership was the factor that weighed heavily in planning the arrangement of the plot.

The dwelling units—of five types ranging from bachelor singles to 3 bedroom plus study units—were grouped to form a series of courts where children at play may be watched. All dining-kitchen and living rooms face the courts for this reason, as well as for favorable outlook upon no-traffic areas. Bachelor units (designated B) are placed on the periphery, closing the courts at these points and providing convenient access to the Institute dining facilities across the road. Note that the courts are not closed quadrangles but are suggested enclosures, free at their corners and visually open where carports cut through the buildings.

The focus for the plan is the common, or "village green," dedicated to adults and community affairs. It is ringed by the main access road, called Einstein Drive. Through travel is discouraged by bending or narrowing through roads; service traffic is kept away from courts. Where units are shown dotted, several existing cottages will remain temporarily for added housing, community use, and expansion.

The natural configuration and character of the land were carefully maintained; trees were saved wherever possible. Buildings were placed with their lengths paralleling existing contours in order to minimize excavation and grading.

Architect: Marcel Breuer; Associate, Robert Gatje. Engineers: Slocum & Fuller, Consulting; Wiesenfeld, Hayward & Leon, Structural. Landscape Architect: Bryan J. Lynch. Builders: Sovereign Construction Co.

Continental Air Views'

In the aerial views above, one can see the Institute building in the foreground, lower picture; the new housing across the road, center; and the golf course beyond, top. The town of Princeton and the University lie in the distance beyond the golf course—roughly a 10-minute drive away.

AREA COMPUTATION—All Areas Gross

TYPE	UNITS	SQ.FT./UNIT	SUB-TOTAL	USE
A	1	980	980	Caretaker's Apt., 3 BR's
B	32	515	16,480	Single Occupancy with Kitch.
C	20	755	15,100	LR, K-Dining, 1 BR, Study
D	20	1,035	20,700	LR, K-Dining, 2 BR's, Study
E	24	1,035	24,840	LR, K-Dining, 2 BR's, Study
F	10	1,130	11,300	LR, K-Dining, 3 BR's, Study

RECAPITULATION

Floor Areas, 107 Living Units	89,400 sq ft
Porches and Carports	24,900 sq ft
Service Areas (Laundry, Boiler)	4,400 sq ft
TOTAL PROJECT	118,700 sq ft

Type C; ground floor at left, upper floor at right

Ben Schnall

Type E; one-story unit

Type D; ground floor at left, upper floor at right

At the beginning of the design process, dwellings in a variety of shapes were considered, but the decision was for the restful horizontality of one and two-story row houses; modified from the conventional to rob them of the monotony so often associated with that kind of building. This was accomplished by means of changing roof overhangs, sunshades, screen and terrace walls of contrasting

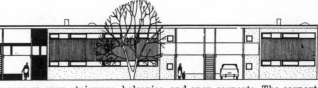

masonry, open stairways, balconies, and open carports. The carports prove especially effective in breaking the "row" impression, and as they occur, provide vistas through and beyond the houses. Also, their roof decks serve double duty as porches for the occupants of the upper floor at that location. There are five types of apartments, B through F, and they are shown on these two pages by means of the

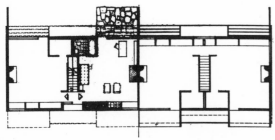

Type B; ground floor at left, upper floor at right

architect's presentation plans and elevations. The type A unit—of which there is only one—is pictured on the following page; a tabular summary of the occurrence and areas of types is printed on the preceding page.

Study of the plans will reveal certain features—unusual in the design of institutional housing—that are common to all the apart-

Type F; one-story unit

ments. In a given unit, all the rooms are on one level; the living room and dining-kitchen areas open to the garden court, either by terrace or protected balcony; the dining area is adjacent to the living room, either opening to it or screened off; the bedrooms are of sufficient size to accommodate two beds plus an area for study; the study proper is designed to be used alternately as a bedroom

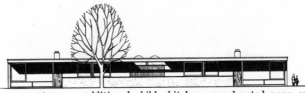

for a guest or an additional child; kitchens are located near entrance doors; and every apartment boasts a fireplace!

On the exterior, high strip windows in the entrance façades of the buildings provide privacy for the rooms facing this way; and sun protection is furnished either by roof overhangs or wood louvers for all glass areas that are exposed to strong sunlight.

207

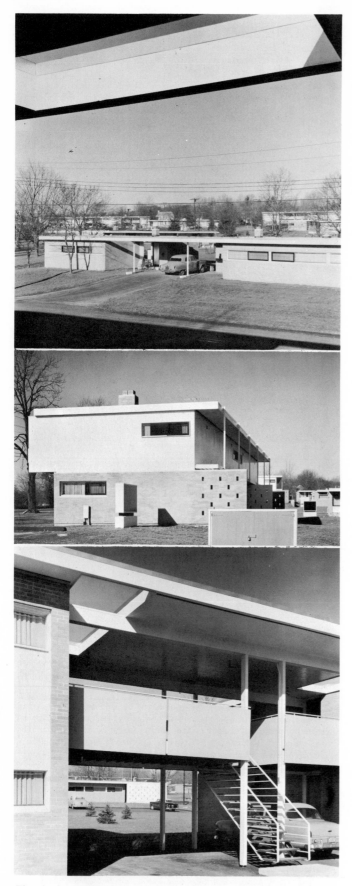

A fireplace for each apartment

The single type A unit, top, houses the superintendent's apartment and central heating plant. A typical carport is shown above.

Exterior materials and colors: light orange-rose brick; natural cedar siding; trim and fascias painted white with black accents; free-standing electric distribution boxes variously painted in vivid colors. The construction is conventional wood frame with brick veneer; the sliding sash are of special design.

Type E, court side

Type B, bachelor unit

All photos by Ben Schnall

Type F, entrance side

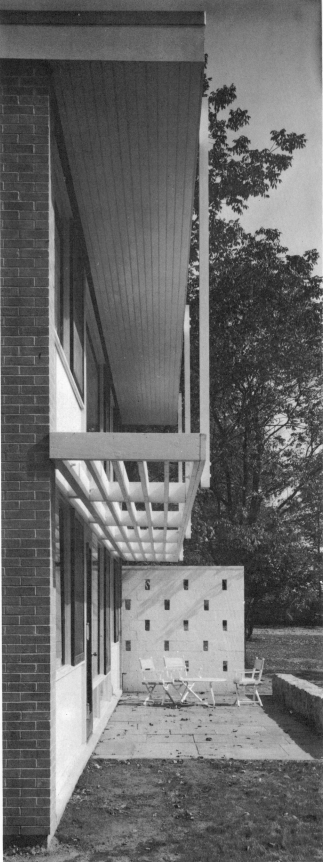

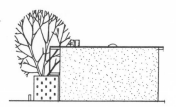

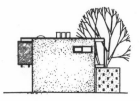

One can note, in the above picture of a typical terrace, how screen-walls of concrete block are employed to secure privacy. The block—which are painted light gray—are laid in a pleasing pattern of solids and voids that robs the screen of apparent heaviness. The louvered sunshade—in addition to serving its prime function—lends also a feeling of shelter to the terrace space.

Marcel Breuer, Architect

Cooperative Dormitory

Vassar College

Poughkeepsie, New York

AN ARCHITECTURE OF ENERGY

IN AN OLD COLLEGE SETTING, with its venerable buildings, this new dormitory has a quality that almost makes it jump. There was no attempt here to make it blend with its ancient neighbors, not even any urging that it do so. The desire was rather to assert the "floating, still uncrystallized energies" of a college group, to create something felt, not merely seen.

Breuer has taken pains with laymen to explain that form-follows-function is inadequate explanation of this particular form, though hastening to add that the functional approach is assumed to be a simple necessity in any building problem, up to a certain point.

In this instance the analysis went: there should be privacy for the bedrooms; one way to achieve this is to elevate them from the ground. Two gains follow: covered outdoor areas for ping-pong tables, games, bicycles, and uninterrupted views, so that the building does not split its site quite so sharply, or seem to crowd its campus.

The living-dining portion does sit on the ground, giving the dormitory a binuclear scheme that separates, actually and psychologically, the noise, music and traffic of this area from the relative quiet of the study-bedrooms.

Bedrooms, besides being elevated, should be sunny: thus the orientation of windows is east-west. There should be protection from hot midday sun, hence the sunshades. Office, utility room, upstairs lounge, telephone booth and bathrooms should be along the central path of traffic, to reduce disturbance and nervosity as well as mere number of steps.

Most of the bedrooms are for double occupancy, though they are partially compartmentalized so that one girl may sleep while the other studies.

If this analysis determines form, how say what determines esthetics? Breuer has made a thrust at it in this (his first and only poem):

"Often you ask: where and how and what are esthetics, beyond functions needed?

Colors which you can hear with ears,

Sounds to see with eyes,

The void you touch with your elbow,

The taste of space on your tongue,

The fragrance of dimensions,

The juice of stone."

Which is probably as good a way as any to explain an architecture that is not to be seen in one plane, but must be experienced.

Whether Breuer builds into his site or onto it is a question that will not be settled by the Vassar Dormitory, for this building has the familiar Breuer low-seat walls to merge site and building, also the frank elevation of one portion above ground. Maybe this building suggests an answer to a current academic argument which has generated many thousands of words

Joseph Molitor Photos

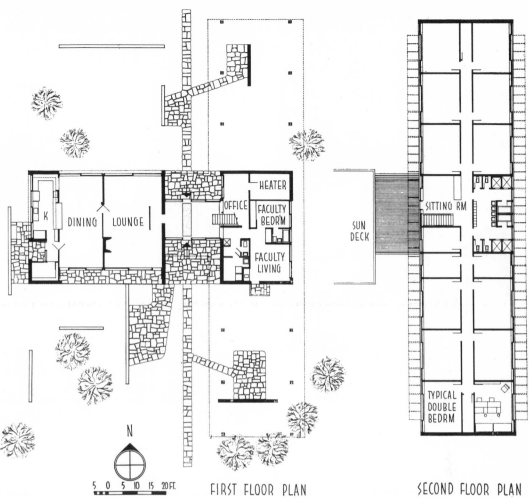

HEATER

OFFICE

FACULTY
BEDR'M

K   DINING   LOUNGE

FACULTY
LIVING

SUN
DECK

SITTING RM

TYPICAL
DOUBLE
BEDRM

N

5   0   5   10   15   20 FT.

FIRST FLOOR PLAN

SECOND FLOOR PLAN

Joseph Molitor Photos

Breuer's Vassar Dormitory is a cooperative house in which the girls do their own work, even the cooking. Efficiency exhibits itself in kitchen and serving arrangements, but by no means dominates the interiors. The living-dining area presupposes a good measure of energy and noise, and is set apart from the strictly dormitory portion so that exuberance need not be inhibited. The glass walls do more than ''bring the outside in,'' there is perhaps a suggestion of letting the inside out. At any rate, these interiors are designed to be open, with a calculated note of gaiety

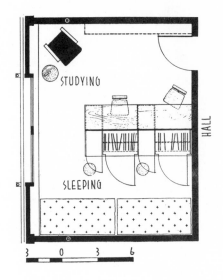

Upper photograph shows the up-stairs lounge where the girls may break the grind for that all-important chatter. It is located right at the head of the stairs, opens to roof deck beyond. View in center is one of the single rooms; note the panel in the convector cover; holes may be closed for heat control by just sliding the panel. Photograph at left shows living room of special apartment for the faculty adviser

Typical double bedroom is divided into sleeping space and study space by head-high cabinet partition. On one side are aligned two study desks, each with inset lighted panel. Other side of this same fixture lights dressing table in sleeping portion

The fun of structural things in tension here comes out in a cable stabilizer for the pipe-supported sunshades. Shade itself is sections of corrugated asbestos cement, with small spaces between sections to make light stripes across the building

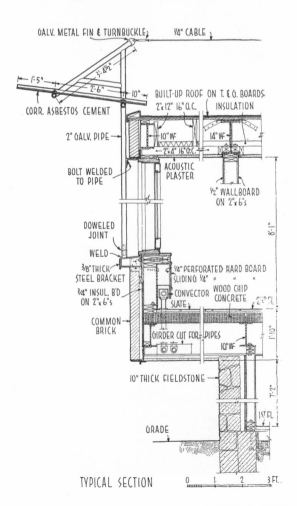

GALV. METAL FIN & TURNBUCKLE   ¼" CABLE

CORR. ASBESTOS CEMENT

2" GALV. PIPE

BOLT WELDED TO PIPE

BUILT-UP ROOF ON T. & G. BOARDS
2"x12" 16" O.C.   INSULATION

10" WF   14" WF

2"x4" 16" O.C.

ACOUSTIC PLASTER

½" WALLBOARD ON 2"x6's

DOWELED JOINT

WELD

⅜" THICK STEEL BRACKET

¾" INSUL. B'D ON 2"x6's

¼" PERFORATED HARD BOARD SLIDING ¼" "

CONVECTOR

WOOD CHIP CONCRETE

SLATE

COMMON BRICK

GIRDER CUT FOR PIPES

10" WF

10" THICK FIELDSTONE

GRADE

1ST FL.

TYPICAL SECTION   0   1   2   3 FT.

WOMEN'S DORMITORY QUADRANGLE

ARIZONA STATE COLLEGE, TEMPE, ARIZ. | *Guirey & Jones, Architects* | *J. E. Hastain, Structural Engineer* | *M. M. Lowry, Mechanical, Electrical Engineer* | *Mary Louise McLeod, Color Consultant*

SIMPLE NEARLY TO AUSTERITY yet serene and most pleasant, Gammage Annex, the new women's dormitory at Arizona State, surrounds three sides of a quadrangle whose present attractiveness is due to increase as grass and trees become better established. The existing building forms the fourth side of the quadrangle, which the three wings of the Annex do not quite enclose.

Stuart Weiner

Stuart Weiner

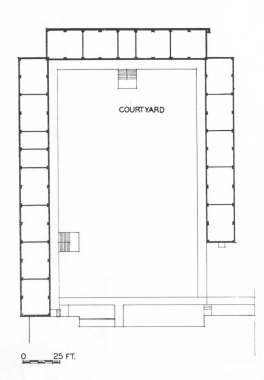

COURTYARD

0   25 FT.

All three wings turn their backs, punctuated only by high rows of windows, on the rest of the campus. Into the privacy of the court, however, all the rooms open hospitably across wide balconies that serve as both sunshades and corridors. There is no waste in this design, and on the other hand it is by no means a concession to poverty. Though the building is liberally enhanced with color, which undoubtedly increases its femininity, the satisfaction it affords depends primarily on the logical disposition — and even exposure — of its elements.

The design module, a four-person dormitory unit (see following pages), is expressed in the plan at left, where the sound-resistant partitions of pumice block are indicated. Upper floors in both two- and three-story wings are similar.

Construction was equally simple and economical. The frame is steel, in bays that are completely repetitive. Floor slabs and roof deck, which cantilever to form the balconies, are concrete. The roof is built-up, with a heat-reflecting surface. Outer walls, except on quadrangle sides, are iron spot face brick. Partitions between units, and spandrels on the court sides, are painted pumice block; other interior partitions are painted plywood. Glazed structural tile is used in baths. Ceilings are vermiculite plaster; floors, asphalt tile. Sash are wood, in station-wagon guides. Insulation is mineral wool. Heating is provided by the college plant; air washers were built specially.

The three wings open generously to the interior quadrangle. The concrete floor and roof slabs overhang to serve as balconies, sunshades and corridors; there are no internal corridors. The unity and privacy of the quadrangle are enhanced by the narrow strip-windows which the dormitory presents to the outer world

The dormitory unit, extremely simple and economical of space, with pleasantly colorful painted block and plywood wall surfaces, is the building's module. It consists of two double bedrooms and two studies paired about a utility wall. Against this wall in each bedroom is a recess containing two built-in dressers with a lavatory set into the counter-top. A single bathroom, containing shower and water closet, is accessible from both bedrooms. Beds are springs and mattresses on a lumber base. Only portable furniture: two chairs per desk

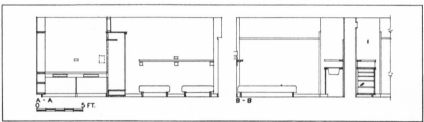

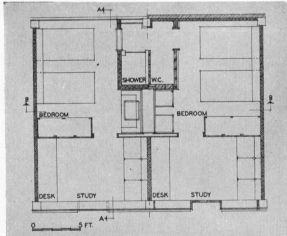

Study has double built-in desk

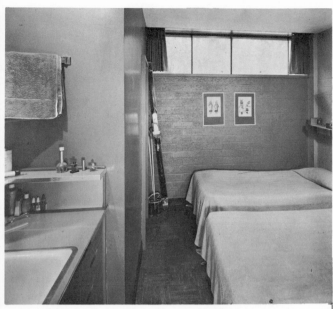

Looking through bath

Bedroom; utility wall at left

Above, wardrobe forms wall between bedroom and study, below

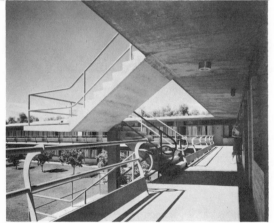

Stuart Weiner

DORMITORY, KISKIMINETAS SPRINGS SCHOOL

SALTSBURG, PA.   *Hunter, Caldwell & Campbell, Architects*

At FORWARD-LOOKING KISKI preparatory school, the new dormitory is as interesting as the plan of study. On this wooded campus the boys concentrate on a single subject for nine weeks, cover four subjects each year, with results gratifying to both teachers and pupils.

Equally successful is this dormitory, the realization of such design studies as the model shown in the photograph at right. The overall building program for the future includes five more such dormitories, a field house, chapel, and dining commons. The present unit has a glass-walled lounge on the ground floor which yields a vista through the building. Also on the ground floor are faculty apartments and activities rooms.

Second and third floors contain two-room apartments for 64 boys, four to a suite, 32 to a floor. The above-ground location achieves privacy and affords pleasant views. Finishes are practical and economical: acoustic tile ceilings, painted block walls, asphalt tile floors. Beds are double-decker; dresser, wardrobe, bookcases are built-in.

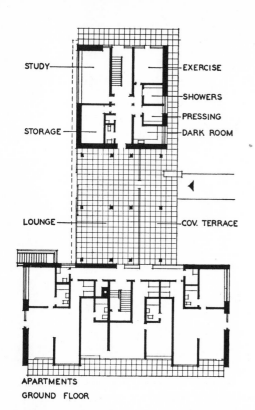

STUDY
EXERCISE
SHOWERS
PRESSING
STORAGE
DARK ROOM

LOUNGE
COV. TERRACE

APARTMENTS
GROUND FLOOR

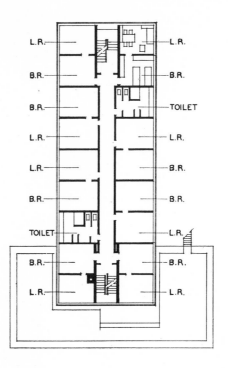

L.R. — — L.R.
B.R. — — B.R.
B.R. — — TOILET
L.R. — — L.R.
L.R. — — B.R.
B.R. — — B.R.
TOILET — — L.R.
B.R. — — B.R.
L.R. — — L.R.

FIRST FLOOR

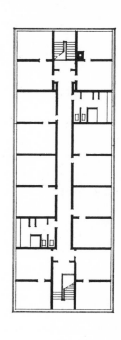

SECOND FLOOR

Exterior skin of upper stories is blue-green glass in aluminum frames, with projected sash for ventilation. Frame is light steel; floors are radiant heated concrete slabs. Photos at right: faculty apartments, easily accessible, control students' comings and goings

Robert Lautman

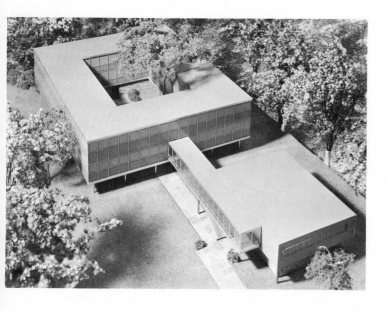

225

ILLINOIS INSTITUTE OF TECHNOLOGY, CHICAGO

RESIDENCE HALLS

Ludwig Mies van der Rohe, Architect

Pace Associates, Associated Architects

Dr. JOHN T. RETTALIATA, President of Illinois Tech, pointed out in the course of an address recently that Chicago's mid-America location, in addition to making it the world's greatest industrial city, had in the past enabled it to lead the country architecturally; he suggested that the city's vitality as well as its situation could attract talent and patrons of all the industrial arts. Illinois Tech's newly developed 110-acre campus in Chicago's industrial south side thus has a positive goal and a continuing philosophy.

Carman Hall, recently completed student-staff apartment building

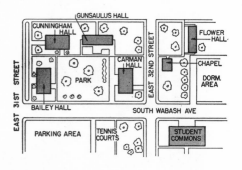

Plot plan shows residential campus; right, part typical plan, Cunningham and Bailey Halls; layouts vary slightly. Cunningham will have 6, 5 and 2-room units (total, 56), Bailey, 4, 3 and 2-room units (total, 88), for married students and staff

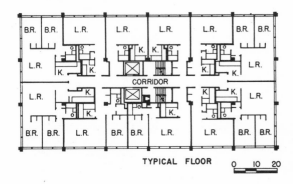

TYPICAL FLOOR   0   10   20

Lobby, Carman Hall

Typical apartment, Carman Hall

Hedrich-Blessing

Index

A

B

C

H

I

J

K

L